SURVIVING THE GLOBAL
FINANCIAL CRISIS

Other Books by the Same Author

Agenda: A Plan for Action (1971)

Exit Inflation (1981)

Jobs For All: Capitalism on Trial (1984)

Canada at the Crossroads (1990)
(Le Canada à Son Carrefour)

Damn the Torpedoes (1990)

Funny Money:
A Common Sense Alternative to Mainline Economics (1994)

SURVIVING THE GLOBAL FINANCIAL CRISIS

THE ECONOMICS OF HOPE FOR GENERATION X

PAUL HELLYER

Chimo Media

Canadian Cataloguing in Publication Data

Hellyer, Paul, 1923-
  Surviving the global financial crisis

Includes bibliographical references and index.
ISBN 0-9694394-3-1

1. Macroeconomics. 2. Economic history – 1990-
3. Economic policy. I. Title.

HC59.15.H45 1996   339.5   C95-933220-0

Printed and bound in Canada. The paper used in this book is acid free.

Chimo Media Limited
99 Atlantic Ave., Suite 302
Toronto, ON M6K 3J8
Canada (416) 535-1008

CONTENTS

FOR

GENERATION X

ACKNOWLEDGMENTS

As always, I am deeply grateful to a number of individuals and organizations for their assistance in the preparation of this book. I am indebted to Susan Bellan, the late Bill Bussiere, Jordan Grant, Wm. Hixson, Bill Krehm and professors John Hotson and W.H. Pope for reading part or all of the manuscript. Their insightful suggestions were of immense value both in respect of content and as to the manner in which the material might be presented. They also helped me to avoid the inevitable errors and omissions. Responsibility for those that slipped through the net, and for the positions taken, rest with me alone.

My able research assistant, Jan Mathys Willems, proved to be an invaluable resource. He was able to trace and find the most illusive information. He also prepared the tables and figures which help illustrate some of the most important points in my thesis.

Nina Moskaliuk, my executive assistant, deserves a special word of praise. She was painstaking in her research and verification of facts and references as well as indefatigable in recording and revising the text chapter by chapter.

Rachel Mansfield earned my appreciation for preparing the index with meticulous care.

A number of organizations were especially cooperative and gracious in lending assistance. These include the parliamentary library in Ottawa, the John Robarts and Metro Reference libraries in Toronto, the United States Consulate in Toronto and the United Kingdom High Commission in Ottawa. To each and all my grateful thanks.

Finally, I would like to thank my family one more time. I realize that they, and especially my wife Ellen, have borne the considerable cost of my lifelong obsession with macro-economic policy and my determination to share my beliefs with a wider audience.

INTRODUCTION

"A person who has ceased learning ought not to be allowed to wander around loose in these dangerous times."

Anonymous

Imagine that you are living 2000 years ago in a small town on the shores of the Mediterranean Sea. You have never been more than a few miles from your place of birth. You know that the world is flat because that is the way it appears to you and there is no reason to believe otherwise.

Then, one day, someone comes along and says that in their opinion the world may not be flat – it may, in fact, be spherical. You nod knowingly because you wish to appear polite. But when that person's back is turned you roll your eyes as a signal that you suspect some sort of mental aberration.

That is the way most people react to economic radicals. Ask a friend if they know why we had a Great Depression in the 1930s and did it need to happen? Or why have there been a number of recessions since the end of World War II, including the last two devastating ones in 1981-82 and 1990-91, and were they really necessary? Usually their eyes will glaze over as a signal that they have switched channels. Yet these are the questions that are relevant to the warp and woof of their daily lives.

Why are we so much further in debt today than we were 20 years ago? Is it entirely due to government overspending or are there other reasons – a vast increase in the cost of money, for example? And why is the landscape so bleak that a whole generation of young people are being conditioned to believe that their future will be less bright than the one enjoyed by their parents? Does this bleak prospect make sense when the physical potential of the real economy has never been greater?

Something is desperately wrong – something even more fundamental than governments' seeming inability to balance budgets and their increasing powerlessness in the face of vast quantities of stateless capital acting as international vigilantes discipling anyone who strays from the financial market's narrow perception of what is right and what is wrong. Surely it is a form of wrong when nameless, faceless international financiers can veto the will of nation states as expressed by their constitutionally elected leaders.

This churning cauldron of capital, which is to finance what the atomic bomb is to warfare, is just one of the demons that political leaders must exorcize. They must also break the intellectual shackles of an irrational monetary and banking system – a system which, if stripped of all the snake oil and holy water that has been poured on it over the years, is little more than the perpetuation of a scam practiced by the English goldsmiths more than three hundred years ago. It is an unjust and unsustainable system which has put the world in hock up to its ears and which has to be reformed if capitalism is to survive and prosper.

It is my unshaken opinion, after half a century of study and concern, that there has never been a depression or a recession that was necessary. They have all been, basically, monetary phenomena flowing from a system that was never planned and which just grew like topsy. Two hundred years after James Watt's adaptation of the steam engine and the industrial revolution changed, for all time, the order of magnitude of the potential for producing goods, economists still haven't designed a complementary system of distribution. Mainline economists haven't managed to negotiate and safely exit from the labyrinth of change. They are still lost in the maze of mirrors.

Don't get me wrong. Many great economists have played on the world stage and deserve their recognized place in history. I have read dozens of their most important works and have often been in total awe of the formidable intellects of the authors. Their mastery of microeconomics is unquestioned and of immense value in attempting to understand the subject.

When it comes to macroeconomics, however, there is less consensus. I am equally awestruck by the complicated mathematical formulae and the ingenious abstractions of specialists in this field. When I put their books down, however, I think how detached most of them are from the real world of political economy. Generation after generation goes by and we still don't have a theory, or combination of theories, which will allow us to achieve and maintain full employment in the absence of significant inflation. Indeed many economists, influenced more by economic history than mathematical certainty, deny that such a state is possible – except, perhaps, in the short run. So central banks, encouraged by mainline economists, have institutionalized this view to the detriment of wealth creation.

To confirm this opinion I read *The Fortune Encyclopedia of Economics* to refresh my memory. The brief summaries of the major schools of thought, though interesting, left me with that same empty feeling that I have felt for so long. The neoclassical, new classical macroeconomics and monetarist schools can all be dismissed as inadequate because they are based on a hypothetical "price-auction" economy which, to the extent it may have existed at one time, has long since ceased to exist. They offer no hope and no solutions for the real economy.

Keynesian and neo-Keynesian models are closer to reality when they accept the downward stickiness of wages and prices; but they, too, have failed to recognize the preponderant influence of monopoly power as the source of contemporary inflation. This results in a tolerance of involuntary unemployment which is unnaturally and unnecessarily high. In addition, Keynesians, like their classical, neoclassical and monetarist homologues, have failed to address the monetary and banking issues which are leading to an unsustainable burden of debt. In effect, then, there is no major economic school offering workable solutions to the real problems of the real economy. Little wonder that young people, sensing that this is true, have been losing hope.

Fundamental to the problem is that economics is very much like theology. If the prevailing theory says that the sun revolves around the earth, the sun revolves around the earth. Rational discussion is neither encouraged nor welcome. It's the economic "seminarians" against the world.

About twenty years ago I sent an outline of a book on economic reform to Doubleday in New York in the hope they would agree to publish it. Several weeks later I received a letter of rejection which stated: "Our editors believe that the economists can't all be wrong." Throughout the years I have mused that had Galileo sent Doubleday an outline of his thesis that the earth revolves around the sun he would have received a letter back saying: "Our editors believe that the bishops can't all be wrong." History will show that, notwithstanding the judgment of Doubleday editors, mainline economists have failed us miserably and that millions of people have suffered, needlessly, as a result.

In contrast to mainline economics there have always been a few mavericks on the macroeconomic side who deserve a special place in heaven for their pioneering efforts; and there are some living today who have been fighting a courageous lopsided battle in an attempt to persuade the world to listen. They deserve a special award for valor because they have been perceived as the lunatic fringe of economics when in fact they have been the precursors of economic sanity. Some of them have been a great source of support and encouragement to me in writing this book.

Apart from monetary theory, one of the most grievous errors of mainline economics has been its insistence that cost-push inflation be fought by monetary means, that is, by means of tight money and high interest rates. There has been precious little discussion of alternatives. For more than two decades I have been proposing a simple but potentially effective incomes policy as a gentler, fairer way of controlling the wage-price spiral than the horrendous recessions we have been forced to endure. In a sentence, it is the imposition of guidelines to limit the abuse of monopoly power on the part of big business and big labor. Had the suggestion been implemented prior to the last two major recessions, as an alternative to the monetarist approach which has been comparable to using a bulldozer instead of a hoe to weed a flower garden, it would have been possible to achieve acceptable levels of employment and balanced budgets without significant inflation. The situation today would have been as summer compared to winter – though still less than ideal.

Now, however, with the near-universal increase in deficits and debt, more heroic measures are required. For the first time since the Great Depression of the 1930s non-revolutionary measures appear to be inadequate. Forget the federal debt for a moment. Federal debts and deficits, though important, are being used as red herrings to divert attention from more fundamental issues. Total debt in the U.S. today – the sum of personal, corporate, and governmental debt at the federal, state and municipal levels – is approximately 200% of gross domestic product. Even more alarming, the average interest rate on that debt is much higher than the projected growth rate of the economy. You don't need a PhD in economics to know that if you owe twice as much as you earn, and the interest rate on what you owe is far greater than your annual increase in income, you are headed for trouble with a capital T. The system, as presently constituted, is unsustainable. It will certainly crash. The only unanswered question is when the crash will occur.

The extent of the change in course required to salvage the best aspects of capitalism is enormous – about 180 degrees – greater, by far, than anything undertaken since World War II. The monetary system must be fundamentally transformed. The high-flying gaggles of stateless money must have their wings clipped. In addition wage-push inflation must be limited by some means other than by raising interest rates and curtailing output.

The objective must be a proper marriage between the financial economy and the real economy of goods and services. The importance of the marriage was underlined in a March 14, 1994 *New York Times* article entitled "Big Economies Turn to the Jobs Issue", in advance of the first Group of Seven financial conference ever to include labor ministers. It read, in part: "We used to think that jobs and the economy were the same thing," the United States Secretary of Labor, Robert B. Reich, said: "But we have learned in recent years that the paper economy and the people's economy are not always the same thing."

Indeed they are not! But the most significant aspect of Mr. Reich's statement is recognition of that fundamental fact. To the best of my knowledge it was the first time anyone of cabinet rank publicly acknowledged that there are two economies and that one may be hopelessly out of sync with the other.

A marriage contract between the two economies, then, is the bed-rock on which I will build. Friends familiar with my work will know that for the chapters on economic analysis and the incomes policy I have borrowed extensively from previous books on the same subject. Much of the material on monetary reform was first published in *Funny Money: A Common Sense Alternative to Mainline Economics*, in 1994. This book broadens the debate to include the dubious and increasingly disastrous role of central banks. Instead of laying the foundation for a sane and prosperous tomorrow, they have set a course which will lead the world economy to an inevitable meltdown. To give them the absolute autonomy from governments and parliaments that they now seek would be to signal "game over" before it has begun.

Is it too late to avoid the catastrophe? Theoretically not, if action were swift and decisive – as improbable as that may be. But the sirens should be sounded in the hope that someone will hear despite the noisy cacophony of conventional wisdom. The majority has been brainwashed to believe that the economic degeneration of the last two decades was inevitable; that we are helpless in the face of the new global realities; and that the change is irreversible. Happily these widely accepted "truths" are all false. The current retrenchment didn't need to happen; it doesn't have to continue; and it is still reversible if public policy-makers would start asking the right questions.

I make no apology, therefore, for writing to a primarily American audience. The Federal Reserve Board's policies, and philosophy, fill me with foreboding. It is not just the U.S. economy that is at stake but the world economy, including that of Canada. Our rowboat is tied to "U.S.S. CALAMITY" which is headed straight into the rocks. If the Fed and other central banks stay the course there will be one more horrendous accident that didn't need to happen.

There are alternatives worth exploring and I propose to discuss some of them in this book. Anyone who has a limited interest in economics may wish to skip chapters 2 and 3 because they are primarily for people who like to debate issues like the origin of inflation. In other chapters readers may detect a certain amount of duplication. This is not inadvertent. Some of the points are of sufficient importance that they have to be stated over and over again.

On the other hand I must admit that on a subject so incredibly complex I have not included all the permutations and combinations that test every general proposition. To do so would be tedious for me and deter far too many potential readers from persisting to the end. I must be forgiven, too, for failing to bow the knee to political correctness. My knees are not as supple as they once were and what I have to say is designed to benefit everyone without distinction of group, race, gender or class. My goal is to provide a ray of hope for all. If generation X will make the effort required to understand the issues, and then pledge not to vote for anyone who doesn't understand, there will be hope for a brighter tomorrow.

CHAPTER 1

MONETARISTS AND THE CHICAGO SCHOOL BLEW IT!

"The world we have made as a result of the level of thinking we have done thus far, creates problems we cannot solve at the same level of thinking at which we created them."

Albert Einstein

Let's face it, the monetarist counter-revolution of the last twenty years has been one monumental flop. This was inevitable because monetarism is a hothouse plant bred and nurtured in the esoteric garden of the Academy. It was never suitable for transplanting directly into the real economy where, despite its cosmetic innocence, it would have the same smothering effect demonstrated by the Purple Loosestrife when transported from Europe to the swamps of North America. It crowded out everything traditional and worthwhile.

It is true that "practical monetarism", as former Federal Reserve Board Chairman Paul Volcker called the variety that he planted in the real world, reduced the level of inflation substantially and dampened the inflationary expectations that had raised their ugly head. But at what cost? The implementation of monetarism has created more financial turbulence than we have seen at any time since World War II. It has induced two horrendous recessions, slowed economic growth, produced unconscionable levels of unemployment and raised the debt burden to the point where the world economy is set on a collision course with disaster. Thanks to "practical monetarism" the world financial system is headed for a melt-down.

"CAPTAIN" VOLCKER TAKES COMMAND

It is easy to understand Paul Volcker's initial pre-occupation with inflation. U.S. prices had been relatively stable from 1950 to 1965 when they began to escalate. The pace quickened throughout the 70s and reached double-digit proportions by the end of the decade. Federal Reserve Board Chairman Arthur F. Burns, and his temporary successor G. William Miller, had been either unwilling or unable to rein in the monetary growth that was fuelling the inflationary fire. Confidence was being undermined and investors began to put their money into gold, silver, real-estate, art, rare stamps and other artifacts likely to hold their value against a debased currency. Obviously something had to be done.

The man of the hour was Paul Adolph Volcker, President Jimmy Carter's nominee, who took the helm at the Fed on August 6, 1979. Volcker was a big man physically, 6'7", with big plans for change. He had been influenced by Professor Milton Friedman and the Chicago school of monetarists who championed the notion that prices can only rise as fast as the money supply. Consequently all that was necessary to achieve price stability was to limit the growth in the supply of money – or monetary aggregates as the economists call it – to the same percentage as the growth in the real economy.

When Volcker told the then Treasury Secretary George Miller and the President's Council of Economic Advisers chairman Charles Schultze that he proposed to apply strict monetary targets to the banking system they were strongly opposed because they thought that was the road to recession. They were right, and the subsequent recession was a contri-buting factor in Carter's electoral defeat in November, 1980. But Volcker was undeterred by politics. He began by engineering an increase in the Fed's discount rate, the imposition of an 8 percent reserve requirement on increases in Eurodollar borrowings and other managed liabilities which the banks were using as ingenious ways to circumvent their reserve requirements and, finally, a change in operating procedures, i.e., the imposition of monetary targets instead of interest rate targets.

It wasn't enough. Despite a 2½% jump in the Fed Funds rate from 11.5 percent to 14 percent, the speculative lending boom continued at an accelerated pace. By January, 1980, inflation soared to an astronomical 17 percent as financial markets ignored the stringent medicine. In explaining the phenomenon Salomon Brothers' Henry Kaufman said that practical monetarism "occurred against the backdrop of a market that now had floating rates in it and adjustable rate mortgages, a prime loan rate that was floating, the advent of floating rate financing in the Euromarket, the beginning of leakages of funds – that is, from one national border through another national border; if you couldn't finance here, you could go to the Euromarket, and so on. All of that meant a substantial escalation in the rate structure."[1]

Volcker persisted. Between February and April, 1980, Fed Funds interest rates were increased from 14 percent to more than 18 percent. The banks raised their prime rates above 20 percent in tandem. When, at the same time, the Fed reluctantly imposed credit controls, at White House insistence, the economy collapsed. Real Gross National Product (GNP) plunged by 9.4 percent in the second quarter while unemployment rose. The money supply, instead of following its planned trajectory, shrank dramatically. The inevitable had happened.

The victory was short-lived, however. Stuck with the rules of doctrinaire monetarism, which leave little room for common sense, Fed Funds plunged nine percentage points to less than 9 percent resulting in both long and short-term interest rates below the 11 percent inflation rate. By midsummer the economy roared back and Volcker, having lost round one, had to begin the fight again. His relentless campaign through the run-up to the 1980 presidential election, when Jimmy Carter fell victim to the Fed-induced distress level, and on through the period before and after the inauguration of president Ronald Reagan, produced the desired (from Volcker's point of view) recession – the worst since the Great Depression of the 1930s.

SOCIAL CONSEQUENCES

The social devastation caused by the 1981-1982 recession has been widely discussed. This included massive unemployment on a scale unknown since the Great Depression; tens of thousands of people losing their homes because they couldn't pay the new, higher interest rates on their mortgages; and thousands of bankruptcies occurring when struggling companies couldn't cope with a combination of slack demand and sharply higher interest payments on their bank loans. The inhumane human consequences of the Fed's action should have been enough to signal that the cure was as bad or worse than the disease. But there were other economic consequences that were even more far-reaching. The world financial system was rocked to its core and changed in ways that haven't yet been reconciled with the real world of political economy.

PAUL VOLCKER, CRISIS MANAGER

Steven Solomon's 1995 epic, *The Confidence Game*, provides a blow by blow exposé of the Volcker term as Chairman of the Federal Reserve Board. It should be required reading for all politicians and public officials with any responsibility for policy-making in the areas of finance and economics. The record reveals a near continuum of crises of one kind or another all directly or indirectly related to the Fed's action in precipitating a great recession by monetary means and propelling interest rates through the economic roof.

In Solomon's words: "The U.S. and world economy of the 1980s was molded by the Olympian struggle between massive $200 billion U.S. fiscal deficits and Volcker's relentless struggle to break the inflationary spiral through monetary policy. That policy mix helped generate record high real interest rates, world recession, the LDC [less developed countries] debt crisis, U.S. financial fragility, the superdollar, record external imbalances, and numerous innovations of the financial revolution."[2]

The story of the years that began with the recession was one of small, regional bank failures; of big bank insolvency due to irresponsible LDC and real-estate loans; of sometimes bickering, sometimes collaborating, and sometimes colluding central bankers attempting to stabilize a fragile system and of hoodwinking the public in the process; of Volcker and his collaborators forcing privately-owned banks to involuntarily make new loans to recalcitrant LDC countries in order to camouflage the banks' own financial peril until the International Monetary Fund, using taxpayers money, could ride to the rescue; of Savings and Loan failures which, together with deposit insurance claims in respect of other private banks, cost taxpayers billions; of attempts to stabilize currency exchange rates – sometimes successful, more often futile, but always rewarding speculators with public funds. It is also a story of close calls with the world financial system periodically teetering on the brink of disaster. Above all, it is a story of central bankers using their privileged position to assume the levers of world economic policy and then to claim that power as an exclusive sovereign right.

At the end of his book Solomon concludes: "As competent as central bankers have been, I find it frightful the extent to which we are relying for the prosperity of the free world economy – and ultimately the stability of democratic society – on the judgment of a handful of expert technocrats who, to tell the truth, are often caught by surprise like the rest of us about the transformations occurring in the economy and financial system."[3] Still he seems to lean in the direction of central bank autonomy as the lesser of evils. This is where we part company. Throughout his whole book there is not one line indicating any serious discussion of alternative policies to control inflation. In my opinion the monetarist theology was, and remains, totally disconnected from the real economy. Paul Volcker, who merely happened to be the "captain" in command, is considered by many commentators to be the greatest of the central bankers and the one for whom monuments should be erected for limiting inflation and putting the world economy on what these commentators wrongly believe to be a more stable economic path. That assessment is subject to the caveat, however, that both the means adopted and the new world economic order are incompatible with political democracy. Not only are many of the trade-offs politically and morally unacceptable, the floating rate debt explosion has set the world economy on a collision course with disaster.

PRICE STABILITY IS GOD

It was in 1974 that central bankers decided that price stability should be their principal pre-occupation. It was a priority which appeared to make sense in the context of a decade which produced double-digit inflation. No one wants to see the purchasing power of their savings eroded on that scale. Price stability cannot be considered in isolation from other economic goals, however. After all, there had been many previous examples of price stability or even falling prices – nearly always associated with economic stagnation or depression. Consequently, notwithstanding its importance, price stability is just one of the economic goals which must be taken into account.

It is somewhat alarming, then, that the single-minded pursuit of price stability was not a political decision but a technocratic one taken by unelected bankers not responsible to an electorate. It was a watershed decision because one of the principal reasons for central banks, presumably, was to protect the public from the wild gyrations of a highly-leveraged credit system alternately creating too much or too little money depending on the happenstance of legal tender available to it. Central banks were expected to even out the peaks and valleys of excess and promote steady, acceptable growth. It is one of the great disappointments of the twentieth century that they have failed in the attempt.

Little seems to have changed since the demise of the gold standard. Instead of protecting the public interest, most central banks have played the role of mother hen to the private banks. Instead of letting them fail when they were naughty, and subjecting them to the same discipline exercised in other sectors of the marketplace, banks have been given a privileged position in the economic hierarchy. With some notable except-ions the Fed has adopted extraordinary measures to keep the big banks operating, even when they were technically insolvent, in the name of the wider public good. The attitude has been that no one wants to see the banking system fail so it is okay to adopt rescue measures even at the expense of dipping into public funds. Indeed, the financial system has become so complex that mother Fed has been forced to extend its benign benevolence to non-banking financial institutions for fear of a chain reaction that would affect the banks.

Bankers have always been vocal supporters of sound money but the current pre-occupation with inflation fighting and deficit reduction is unprecedented since my childhood in the dirty thirties. It's all that our financial papers, financial writers and financiers seem capable of discussing. It is the ultimate idolatry. Throughout the centuries man has built temples to his gods. The Jews built their temple in Jerusalem; the Greeks built the Parthenon in Athens; the Normans built magnificent cathedrals across Europe; but today it is likely to be the head office of a bank that towers over the economic landscape.

A MEAN, SLOW-GROWTH SOCIETY

One of the saddest consequences of the monetarist counter-revolution is its mean-spirited cover-up. In the name of financial orthodoxy people no longer seem to matter. It's me first and others maybe – but only if they're lucky or ruth-less. In its efforts to get Americans off welfare and into productive work within five years the Congress is pursuing a laudable goal. The majority of people on welfare would probably prefer to work if they could match their education with a job opening. But the success of the program depends on more education and more job openings and there is no guarantee that there will be either. Money for education is being cut back and there will not be enough jobs to absorb the additional job-seekers if the Fed is still running the country. Congress can spin its wheels all it wants but the whole deal is just one big charade as long as it concentrates its efforts on deficit reduction alone and abdicates its responsibility for monetary policy which is, by far, the most powerful weapon in the economic arsenal.

TABLE 1

Rates of Growth for Key Economic Indicators: 1948-1993 (in percent)

Economic Indicator	1948-1973	1974-1993

1. GNP or GDP
  * GNP in 1982 dollars
  ** GDP in 1987 dollars
	3.70*	2.28**

2. Per Capita Disposable Income
  * In 1982 dollars
  ** In 1987 dollars
	2.45*	1.32**

3. Average Hourly Earnings
  * In 1982 dollars
  ** In 1987 dollars
	2.19*	-0.73**

4. Average Weekly Earnings
  * In 1982 dollars
  ** In 1987 dollars
	1.84*	-1.06**

5. Median Family Income
  * In 1980-82 dollars
  ** 1974-1992 in 1987 dollars
	2.80*	0.14**

6. Output per Hour per Person
  * Non-farm business sector
  ** 1974-1992
	2.51*	0.83**

7. Output per Man Year
  * GNP per employed person in 1982 dollars
  ** GDP per employed person for 1974-1992
    in 1987 dollars
	1.72*	0.59*

8. Industrial Production	4.64	2.06
9. Manufacturing Production	6.07	2.45
10. Total Non-Agricultural Employment	1.17	1.82
11. Manufacturing Employment	1.00	-0.62
12. Services Employment	2.54	2.95
13. Government Employment* * Federal, state, and local	3.60	1.59
14. Federal Government Employment	1.32	0.45

Sources: Economic Report of the President, 1991, 1994

The September 13, 1995, *Wall Street Journal* carried a rather poignant article by editor Robert L. Bartley.[4] The title "Giving Up on Growth?" tells the story. In effect the U.S. has given up on growth. Since the monetarist counter-revolution conquered the hearts and minds of policy-makers the trend line for growth in the U.S. had fallen from 3.7 percent to 2.5 percent. The former, representing the "golden years" of economics, was a line that represented jobs, rising real incomes and an escape hatch which allowed the poor and immigrants the possibility of rising to the surface of economic opportunity. The 2.5 percent line is one of stagnation, excessive unemployment and the end of the American dream for countless of its citizens. That is the inevitable conclusion from comparing the pre-monetarist performance statistics of the 1948-1973 era with those of the 1974-1993 period as set out in Table 1[5] (previous page).

Yet a continuation of the slow growth 2.5 percent line is the current plan for the future. The Fed and other central banks appear to have abandoned strict monetary targets in favor of what they call a nonaccelerating inflation rate of unemployment, or NAIRU, which for the U.S. is said to be something in the order of 6%. What this means is that the Fed will stamp out growth in excess of 2.5% in the name of price stability. In this scenario the jobs that Congress is counting on as an alternative to welfare will never exist! Why, under these circumstances, the Congress would want to maintain a "hands off" policy toward the Fed as "King" is difficult for an outside observer to understand.

DEBT IS THE DEVIL

Even if one is willing to take a callous attitude toward the welfare of individuals, it is totally irresponsible for legislators and public officials to ignore the impact of the debt burden associated with slow growth and high interest rates. Beginning with the Volcker revolution of 1980-82 total public and private U.S. debt has gone skyward from about 140 percent of GDP to approximately 200 percent of GDP in 1995. (See Figure 1)

U.S. Debt to GDP Levels (1946-1994)

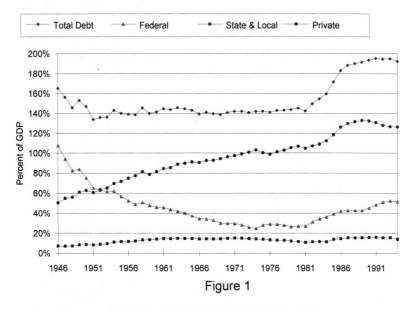

Figure 1

Source: *Flow of Funds Accounts*, Table L2 through L4,
U.S. Federal Reserve Bulletin, from many issues

Worse, there is no prospect of relief. On the contrary, in the absence of radical reform, the problem will just keep compounding until the system crashes under its own debt weight. No one should be misled by the inference that if the federal budget is balanced by 2002 that all will be well and the system will be stabilized. All that will be achieved is off-loading the federal burden on other levels of government, industry and individuals.

A point that must be underlined is the staggering increase in interest rates from the "golden era" 'til now. The only reason that the total public and private debt to GDP ratio in the U.S. was more or less constant in the 140 percent range for 30 years from 1951 to 1981, is that the interest rate on that debt was within shooting distance of the growth rate in the economy. Contrast that with the current situation. As I write, 3-month treasury bills are about 5.25 percent and the 30-year benchmark treasury bond about 6.46 percent, its lowest level in 19 months. The interest on private paper, including credit card balances, is, of course, much higher. There are no accurate figures for the average interest rate on all debt, public and private, but it is unlikely to be less than 2½ to 3 times the Congressional Budget Office projected growth rate of 2.3 percent for the next four years to the end of the millennium.

To illustrate the potential consequences of such a wide spread between interest rates and the growth rate it is useful to do some long-term extrapolations. If you compound the 1994 GDP of $6,736.9 trillion at 2.5 percent for 25 years, and the 1994 total public and private debt of $12,970.5 trillion for the same 25 years, at 6.25 percent, you reach the astounding figures, in 2019, of $12,490 trillion GDP and $59,045 trillion debt – a debt 4.73 times GDP. Even more astounding is a 50 year projection. In the year 2044, GDP would be $23,156 trillion while total public and private debt would be $268,784 trillion, or 11.6 times GDP. If the average rate of interest on that debt were 6.25 percent, annual interest payments would be $16,799 trillion, or 72.5 percent of GDP.

As my friend William F. Hixson said, when he did an even more frightening projection for his book, *A Matter of Interest*, the figures cited above are not a prediction. They are simply a crystal clear signal that current economic trends are unsustainable and that some radical change must occur long before 2044 in order to prevent an economic meltdown.

If you don't like the figures I have arbitrarily chosen try your own. Mine are quite conservative based on the theory of "rational expectations" as expounded by Professor Robert E. Lucas Jr., Nobel laureate for 1995. If anything, based on today's conventional wisdom concerning growth rates and inflation control, I have understated the gravity of what is to come. Which makes one wonder about Professor Lucas' bold assertion at a news conference in Chicago, following news of his prize, that "The U.S. economy is in excellent shape."[6] What is so "excellent" about an economy which is headed for disaster?

No one should pretend that the arithmetic can be ignored. It can't. It is inexorable. A debt burden of approximately 2 times GDP is enough. To keep it from rising it is essential to have growth rates and average interest rates that are equal – a task that, with present policies, is impossible. But as the U.S. Army Service Forces are fond of saying: "The difficult we do immediately. The impossible takes a little longer." There are a series of radical measures that would move us a long way toward that goal. But before considering these propositions in detail it may be worthwhile to consider where the monetarists went wrong. They treated the inflation of the 1970s as though it were a classic inflation of too much money chasing too few goods instead of a new breed of wage-push inflation that was not of great significance in 1949 when Paul Volcker wrote his undergraduate thesis on "The Problems of Federal Reserve Policy Since World War II."

CHAPTER 2

WHERE MAINLINE ECONOMISTS WENT WRONG

*"Economics is Extremely Useful as a Form of
Employment for Economists"*

J.K. Galbraith

The multi-trillion dollar error of mainline economists has been their assumption that the inflation of the last 30 years has been classic inflation, that is, too much money chasing too few goods. It was the case in some countries but not in the highly industrialized Western countries including the United States. With rare and isolated exceptions, like real-estate in a few large urban centers, the blips in energy prices when producers attempted to redress the punitively low prices imposed on them by the world's leading oil companies and the inevitable volatility of other commodity prices, there has been no classic inflation since the end of the Korean War in 1950; no significant shortage of goods and services. The principal cause of inflation in the Western world in the post-Korean War era has been wages rising out of sync with productivity as a result of the monopoly power of big labor and big business.

It is the failure to recognize this fundamental fact that has led monetarists and classical economists to recommend and accept the Draconian measures imposed in 1979 and 1980, and since. Their miscalculation has left economic prospects for the future in shambles. What has been done is comparable to using atomic bombs instead of smart bombs to wipe out a few snipers. The radio-active fallout continues to kill and maim innocents for generations to come. Consequently this chapter and the next will revisit some of the most widely-held views about the origin of contemporary inflation, including the "It started with Vietnam" theory, in an attempt to demonstrate that it was a Western-worldwide escalation in nominal wage demands, rather than the Vietnam War and the increase in oil prices, which affected economies so profoundly.

In reading "Key Propositions of Monetarism", as set out in *Monetarist Economics*, by Milton Friedman,[1] I find myself in general agreement with many of the points. These include the relation between the rate of growth of the quantity of money and the rate of growth in nominal incomes; the time lag between the rate of change in monetary growth and the rate of change in nominal incomes, etc. Where we part company completely is where Friedman asserts: "It follows from the propositions I have so far stated that *inflation is always and everywhere a monetary phenomenon* in the sense that it is and can be produced only by a more rapid increase in the quantity of money than in output."[2] Technically true, but only a half truth in the sense that it only tells half of the story. Omission of the other half of the truth has profound implications for both theory and practice.

As the basis of his beliefs, Professor Friedman cites two U.S. experiments in the 1966-1968 period when, in a tug-of-war between fiscal and monetary policy, the latter proved to be the more formidable. He then goes on to say: "My own belief in the greater importance of monetary policy does not rest on these dramatic episodes. It rests on the experience of hundreds of years and of many countries."[3] I share his conviction that monetary policy is by far the most important economic tool – except in certain rare instances such as the Great Depression when it was a combination of fiscal policy and a policy of money creation by government that began to ease us out of the mess monetary policy had got us into. It was grand scale money creation by government plus grand scale government borrowing from individuals and of money created by private banks that got the economy moving in order to wage war. Where Friedman departs from reality is in his assumption that the economy of the second half of the twentieth century is in all material respects similar to that of the hundreds of years of experience in many countries on which he based his theory. It isn't!

The kind of "price-auction" economic model upon which monetarist theory is based never did exist in totality, although it is closer to the reality of the 19th and early 20th centuries than it is to the post-World War II experience. As an incorrigible auction buff I know first-hand what a price auction looks and sounds like. I also know that sometimes there are reserve bids. In the real world there are many prices which are not flexible at all. Drop in at the post office on a slack day and see how much "elasticity" there is in the price of stamps.

It has been this inability to separate the forest from the trees that has led to some highly questionable assumptions about the cause of post-Korean War inflation. In a 1973 article entitled "Prescribing Remedies for Inflation", the late Vincent Bladen, economics professor at the University of Toronto, suggested that there are five basic causes. In addition to monetary inflation, he mentioned government borrowing to finance wars or social programs, business expansion in excess of available savings, the cost-push of rising wages and prices, and finally a world food shortage. If his article had been written a year later, following the dramatic increase in oil prices, no doubt he would have included that as a sixth variety.

Bladen compared the various "causes" of inflation to fever in the human body: "Just as in medicine, it is essential to identify the specific organisms causing the trouble before prescribing the antibiotic known to be effective in controlling that specific organism, so in political economy, it is essential to identify the specific variety of inflation, the specific cause of a particular inflation, before prescribing a remedy."[4]

It does seem sensible to identify the nature of an illness before prescribing a cure. Yet one should not be misled by the medical analogy. Inflation is inflation whether the money supply is increased to pay for wars, to finance buyouts and leveraged takeovers, to finance government deficits, or to maintain a reasonable level of employment in the face of rising costs. It is only for simplicity of analysis that I am dividing it into its two highly recognized categories: demand inflation, defined as too much money chasing too few goods, and cost-push inflation, in which costs push or chase prices (depending on which you think comes first, the chicken or the egg) to ever-higher heights in a never-ending spiral.

THE VIETNAM WAR

Monetarists, in accord with many other economists, insist that all inflation, including cost-push, has its genesis in excess demand. The extent to which this is true is open to serious question. The record suggests that their conclusion may be more intuitive than empirical.

In any event, most U.S. economists trace the origin of the unacceptable inflation of the 70s and early 80s to a surplus of purchasing power generated by the Vietnam War. For example, it is Robert Lekachman's view that President Johnson's escalation of the war drained manpower from civilian output, while "defense-generated incomes simply added themselves to other incomes in the competition for civilian goods."[5] Congress and the White House did not drain off the excess demand through higher taxes until 1968. Meanwhile unions bargained, successfully, to compensate for past inflation and to hedge against future inflation.

This opinion was endorsed by President Carter's Council of Economic Advisers, who wrote, "It was excess aggregate demand during the Vietnam War that drove up the underlying rate of inflation from 1 percent to 4 or 5 percent by the end of the 1960s."[6] Years after the fact, in his 1983 annual report, the Bank of Canada Governor at that time, Gerald Bouey, climbed on that same bandwagon.

The theory was enshrined in the 9th edition of Paul Samuelson's textbook, *Economics*, the bible of budding young

economists. Samuelson noted that "low unemployment rates
– as in the post 1965 boom, when the average dropped below
4 percent – are associated with a quickening of price inflation."[7]
This widely accepted view leaves some very large questions
unanswered. Neither Samuelson nor Lekachman has taken the
trouble to explain why even lower unemployment rates in 1952
and 1953 – the lowest in more than a quarter of a century –
were achieved without any comparable impact on prices. In
fact, the inflation curve at that time was downward.

In addition, the Vietnam theory does not explain what
happened outside the United States. If Governor Bouey was
correct when he said "demand pressures showed up first in the
United States, largely associated with the Vietnam War, and
later elsewhere,"[8] how does he account for the fact that wages
and prices began their steep ascent in Canada and the United
Kingdom more than a year earlier than they did in the United
States?[9] Neither country was significantly affected by American
involvement in Southeast Asia; therefore to conform with the
conventional wisdom their surge in prices should have followed
rather than preceded the one in America.

DEMAND SHOCKS

The "It started with Vietnam" school has been extended
into a general theory in an attempt to explain the ratchet-like
escalation of prices over the fifteen-year period from 1965 to
1980. The Vietnam War is now cited as the first of three major
events that caused the rate of inflation to surge upward.

In his final *Economic Report to Congress*, Jimmy Carter
said the second, which came in the early 1970s, "was associated
with the first massive oil-price increase, a worldwide crop
shortage which drove up food prices, and an economy which
again became somewhat overheated in 1972 and 1973. The
third inflationary episode came in 1979 and 1980. It was
principally triggered by another massive oil-price increase, but
part of the rise in inflation may also have been due to overall
demand in the economy pressing on available supply."[10]

All well and good. No one denies that each of the three shock-waves affected prices. But President Carter went on to explain that "late in each of the three inflationary episodes monetary and fiscal restraints were applied, and at the end of each a recession took place, with rising unemployment and idle capacity."[11] On the basis of classical theory, as well as of Newton's law of gravitation, prices should then have come down to the previous levels. They had adjusted on innumerable occasions in earlier decades, so why not now?

President Carter's hindsight was dead on when he observed: "A set of inflationary causes raises the rate of inflation; when the initiating factors disappear, inflation does not recede to its starting position despite the occurrence of recession; the wage-price spiral then tends to perpetuate itself at a new and higher level .... It is this downward insensitivity of inflation in the face of economic slack that has given the last 15 years their inflationary bias."[12] Correct! What he didn't explain is where the "downward insensitivity" came from.

In reviewing Presidents' reports for those years, and those of their economic advisers, I found periodic temporary shortages of various goods that would explain why an increase in price would occur. I was unable to unearth examples, with the possible exception of energy, where the shortage was sufficiently prolonged to sustain a permanent price rise. Consequently, I find the demand-shock theory, in isolation, untenable.

In rejecting the Vietnam and demand-shock theses, I wish to underline that I am not speaking of other days and other times. The demand inflation generated as an aftermath of war is well documented.[13] Today, however, this is not a relevant factor. World War II and Korea are distant memories, and any effects from the Vietnam War, which were probably overstated, have long since dissipated.

GOVERNMENT DEFICITS

Another frequently cited scapegoat for inflation is government deficits. In a letter to Canada's Prime Minister, in December, 1975, a group of prominent Canadian economists stated that of three domestic causes of inflation, "first is the growth in government deficits: federal, provincial and municipal."[14]   The same opinion is held by many American businessmen and economists.   In *Inflation: Long-Term Problems*, C. Lowell Harriss states that "federal deficits are widely assumed to be a source, perhaps the chief source, of inflation."[15]

This widespread belief is milked to advantage by political parties of all stripes.   Especially for conservatives, everywhere, the "evil" of big budgetary deficits is accepted as faithfully as holy writ.   Nevertheless, as Harriss went on to say: "Such a conclusion is not necessarily accurate.   The Federal Reserve faces no legal or economic compulsion to provide the banking system with extra reserves so that banks can create money (deposits) to buy the additions to federal debt.   The Treasury may go into the capital markets, and by borrowing there, reduce the amounts available for utilities, housing, manufacturing, and other borrowers."[16]

President Reagan's Council of Economic Advisers tacitly acknowledged this distinction in their 1982 report.   "The impact of a specific deficit will vary, however, depending on the conditions that lead to it.   For example, during a recession – as now exists – the borrowing requirements of business and consumers tend to be relatively small.   At such a time a given deficit can be financed with less pressure on interest rates than during a period of growth, when business and consumer demands for credit are increasing.   That is why it is important for the government to reduce the budget deficit in fiscal 1983 and beyond, a period of anticipated rapid economic growth when private investment demands are expected to rise substantially."[17]

Ironically, the monetarist approach to inflation fighting is incompatible with fiscal conservatism.   "During the last year, (1981) better-than-expected progress on inflation has reduced taxable income, slowing the growth of revenues below earlier projections.   The recession has temporarily slowed the growth of the tax base while increasing outlays for employment-related

programs."[18] So to the extent that deficits are really inflationary, much of what has been gained on the monetary swing has
been lost on the fiscal roundabout.   An analysis of the
consequences of the 1981-82 and 1990-91 recessions demonstrates that nothing contributes more directly and more dramatically to an increase in government deficits than the abrupt
decline in revenues caused by inflation fighting through
monetary means.

There are economists who doubt that deficits have been
a major contributor to inflation.   In Canada the conventional
wisdom was effectively challenged by Robert B. Crozier when
he was senior economist for the Conference Board of Canada.
In a 1976 study entitled *Deficit Financing and Inflation: Facts
and Fictions* [19] Crozier showed that, in Canada, deficit financing
had been a negligible factor contributing to inflation. What had
been more important was the increasing proportion of total
output spent by governments. The high taxes required to finance
these expenditures added considerably to unit costs both
directly, as a significant element in prices, and indirectly, by
increasing labor demands for higher wages. Thus government
expenditures have been an important contributor to cost-push
(or tax-push, as some people like to call it) inflation.

Jimmy Carter's advisers entered a note of caution on
the same subject: "If government budget deficits are the cause
of inflation, it should make no difference whether the deficit
occurs at the Federal, State or local level .... The combined
budgets of Federal, State and local governments have either
showed a surplus or a really small deficit during the past two
decades, except during recessions and for two years when
Federal spending on the Vietnam War was at its peak.

"This notion that budget deficits are the chief cause of
inflation also founders on the comparison of budget deficits and
inflation among different countries.   Japan and Germany in
recent years have had much better success in combating
inflation than the United States.   Yet their budget deficits,
especially those of Japan, have been much higher relative to the
size of their economies than has been the case in the United
States."[20]

I have long been convinced that budget deficits are neither the sole nor principal cause of contemporary inflation in Western industrialized economies. There is much evidence to support my conclusion. That said, it doesn't follow that the size of the deficit is unimportant. It depends, as a politician might say, on the circumstances.

President Reagan's Council of Economic Advisers made the categorical assertion that "it is now generally agreed that continued excessive growth in the money supply will cause sustained inflation. Thus, deficits financed by money creation will have persistent inflationary consequences."[21] The second half of the statement is true only in the context of the preamble where the operative word is "excessive". If the growth in the money supply is excessive there will be inflation with or without deficits. If the expansion of the money stock is not excessive the impact of the deficit will depend, as Lowell Harriss suggested, on where the money to make up the shortfall comes from. One has to look at the total expansion of the money supply, and the use to which it is put, in order to evaluate the impact of deficit financing.

If a government increases its deficit to buy another car for the police, the net effect would be the same as if an individual borrowed the same amount of money to acquire a vehicle for his or her own private use. That said, in both cases the impact on the economy would depend on whether the automobile industry was already operating at capacity.

I accept Harriss' conclusion: "If the economy has much unutilized productive capacity, money creation may finance benefits from government spending without loss of either output or price level increases."[22] If, on the other hand, the capacity of the economy is fully utilized, printing more money will be inflationary regardless of whether the extra cash is used for public or private purposes.

THE ENERGY CRISIS

Another diagnosis attributes inflation to the effects of the rapid escalation of oil prices. The world price of oil soared from $3.00 to $11.65 a barrel between October 1, 1973, and January 1, 1974, resulting in American consumer price increases of 75.5 percent for gasoline and motor oil, 247.5 percent for fuel oil and coal, and 40.6 percent for gas and electricity.[23]

Former Treasury Secretary William E. Simon told a Senate Sub-Committee on September 8, 1974, that "the quadrupling of oil prices over the past year, when its effects are fully felt, will have contributed in the range of 5 to 8 percentage points in our wholesale price index." He added that this was about half the increase in the index for the year ending mid-1974.[24] Later statistics put the effects of the oil-price rise in better perspective. Joel Popkin, a staff member of the President's Council of Economic Advisers, said that energy prices to consumers increased 33.5 percent in the year after the cost of imported oil shot upward, while consumer prices as a whole jumped 11.2 percent. Popkin estimated that energy was responsible for just under one-fifth of the increase in the cost of living.[25]

In Canada, where the increase in oil prices was controlled, the energy component of inflation was even less. Conference Board of Canada analysts estimated that, on average, energy contributed about one-tenth of the increase in the Consumer Price Index for the 1975-81 period. Still, politicians used the actions of the oil cartel as an excuse for the inflation they didn't understand and seemed powerless to control. In his January 1980 Report to Congress, President Carter cited oil prices as "the major reason for the worldwide speed-up in inflation during 1979 and the dimming of growth prospects for 1980."[26]

By 1982 the worm had turned. Increased output by non-OPEC countries, including Britain, Norway, and Mexico, combined with slack demand due to conservation measures and the worldwide recession, created an oil glut. Prices turned soft and by the end of the year were exerting downward pressure on the Consumer Price Index.[27]

At an extended meeting in March 1983 the OPEC ministers finally came to grips with the new reality and agreed to an official reduction of $5 a barrel to bring their prices in line with the new world oil price. Today, in 1995, they have difficulty in agreeing on anything. Consequently world oil prices have been trending first downward and then up again. They are not, however, a major factor in consumer price indices.

Reflecting on the impact of oil prices in the 1970s, one might indeed ask why some countries were so much more successful than others. West Germany and Switzerland both import a higher proportion of their oil needs than do the United States and Canada. It would follow that if oil was the major disrupting factor on economic performance, their records should have been poorer than ours. In fact, they were much better.

For a time when the oil-producing and exporting countries had their act together the whole world shook, yet statistics show that the cartel was given far too much blame for a problem that has been, for the most part, domestic in origin.

EXPECTATIONS

Expectations is a mutant of the rational expectations theory and of all explanations for inflation it is the most airy-fairy and mercurial. But, like most ideas, it is not without a germ of truth. Beginning about 1970 when the wage-price spiral began to spin faster and faster, nearly everyone expected, on the basis of what was happening, that the process would continue. So wages and prices began to leap-frog as management and labor anticipated the actions of the other. It was the first time since the Korean War that prices had not followed wages and represented a rational adjustment by business to labor's expected behavior. Both sides had their sails trimmed with the imposition of the 1981-82 credit squeeze but none of this explains why they were sailing above the limit in the first place.

Similarly, one can argue that continued high interest rates in 1995 reflect a rational expectation that the Fed cannot guarantee low inflation except during periods of unreasonably slow growth. Owners of wealth tack on a premium, especially on long-term paper, due to their disbelief that a slow growth policy can be maintained in the long run. None of this explains why the Fed, armed with its monetarist philosophy, and natural rate of unemployment, cannot achieve price stability and acceptable rates of growth simultaneously. It has not in the past, so rational expectations say that it will not in the future. It is rational, therefore, not to be sanguine based on the Fed's performance to date.

PASSING THE BUCK

Finally, when all else fails and economists still feel uneasy about their analyses of contemporary inflation, they take refuge in the popular notion that it is an international problem largely beyond the competence of individual nation states. They argue that the world economy has become so interdependent that it rises and falls like the tides. Any one country is like a cork on the surface, unable to influence its own movement.

The theory is expounded in the Mundell-Laffer Hypothesis.[28] Rather than view the United States or any other economy as closed, with international relationships grafted on, these two economists insist that the only closed economy it makes sense to talk about is the world economy. One cannot understand the U.S. economy from an American perspective; it must be viewed from a global perspective.

Certainly no country is an island unto itself. A severe frost in the coffee plantations of Brazil affects the worldwide price of the aromatic bean. A similar freeze in Florida boosts the price of orange juice in both Canada and the United States. A major wheat shortage in Russia or China influences the market for grain in North America just as surely as does a crop failure at home. A sudden disappearance of the anchovy off the coast of South America creates unforeseen and far-reaching effects on soy-bean prices in the American Midwest.

It is also true that actions in the monetary field in one powerful jurisdiction affect the ability of other countries to pursue an independent course. Excessively high interest rates in Germany have a disruptive effect on economic performance all across Europe as well as on interest rates worldwide. Any gyration in the U.S. price of money lands on Canadian shores with gale force and devastating effect. Canadian vulnerability has been exacerbated by a 1991 revision to the Bank Act which has now eliminated the necessity for cash reserves in the banking system. This robbed the Bank of Canada of its most powerful tool for pursuing a somewhat independent interest rate course based on our very low inflation. The bankers stole our ammunition before the battle began.

As Mundell and Laffer point out, there is evidence that prices, including the price of money, tend to seek a world level. But it is also true that some countries have a much better record in matters of employment and price stability than others and there has been no satisfactory explanation given for these significant variations from the norm.

I admit that no country with an open economy can prevent changes of individual prices affected by world markets. But that doesn't explain or excuse a general rise in prices when the price of oil, lumber, or food goes up. In a free market, with a fixed money supply, some prices must fall when others rise. When people have only so much money to spend and they decide to spend more for one item, then, automatically, they must spend less on something else. Demand for the other item or items declines, and prices should fall accordingly. Consequently, any country in control of its own currency should be able to maintain a constant average price level – at least in theory.

Gerald Bouey, when he was Governor of the Bank of Canada, almost made that point in his 1980 report where he said: "I do not regard increases in the price of one commodity, relevant to another, as a valid reason for a general acceleration of the rate of inflation, because in a less inflationary environment faster-than-average increases in some prices would tend to be offset by slower-than-average increases in others."[29]

If it isn't necessary for the rate of inflation to increase when one price goes up, as the Governor maintained, then by the same logic it should be possible to maintain stable prices. When some prices go up, others should come down. That is how the system should work and would work if we really had a pure market economy. Still, the professionals trot out increases in one commodity as justification for a general price rise. They refuse to admit that we haven't had, don't have, and never will have a "pure" market economy. They just keep pretending that black and gray are white.

CHAPTER 3

THE SCHIZO ECONOMY

*"Both parties join'd to do their best to damn
the public interest."*

Samuel Butler

Modern industrial economies are a mixture of small
and large, public and private enterprise where some prices are
determined by the law of supply and demand and others, including some of the most important ones, are not.   Price-
competitive enterprise operates side by side with natural
monopolies, oligopolies, and trade unions which restrict the
market in labor and render prices inelastic.   A system comprising both free and rigid sectors can be labeled a schizo
economy – one where two very different kinds of enterprise
must co-exist.

Although natural monopolies play a significant role in
the economy, their power and overall economic impact are
minimal in comparison to that of the oligopolies – the inelegant
name that economists have applied to situations where the
market is dominated by a few sellers. Any progressive concentration of market power is likely to end in oligopoly. Important
concentrations have occurred in many industries. Markets for
cereal breakfast foods, cookies and crackers, chocolate and

cocoa products, chewing gum, malt beverages, roasted coffee, cigarettes, pet food, soaps and detergents, explosives, industrial gases, distilled and blended liquors, tires and tubes, gypsum products, flavoring extracts and syrups, sanitary paper products, knit underwear, womens hosiery and myriad other products are dominated by a handful of firms. More than 50 percent of sales accrue to four or fewer companies.[1]

The fact that the concentration has not continued to the point where oligopoly is replaced by monopoly is a benefit that University of Chicago economist and Nobel laureate George Stigler attributes to antitrust laws. He argues that antitrust policies have replaced monopoly and incipient monopoly with oligopoly as the dominant industrial market structure.[2] In *The Economics of Antitrust: Competition and Monopoly*, Richard E. Low says: "This argument can be supported by a host of historical evidence. Oil, tobacco, steel and many other leading products were produced by monopolies, or near monopolies in the early part of this century, until these monopolies were dissolved by the application of antitrust suits or by the passage of time. According to Professor Stigler, and he seems to have logic on his side, time proved as effective as it did only because of the ever-present threat of antitrust. The power of monopolies and of cartels in modern economies without our antitrust policies substantiates this belief."[3]

Whether the difference between U.S. and European experience has been due to the threat of antitrust's big stick, which appears to have become far less fearsome in recent years, or the relative size of the markets is immaterial to most economists' belief that the oligopolies' record in pricing, output, and economic progress is far better than that of monopolies. Even so, that is not to say that they normally engage in the kind of price competition that occurs when there are many sellers. They are far too interdependent.

Professor Richard E. Caves's description of oligopoly underscores the importance of this seller interdependence. "The essence of oligopoly is that firms are few enough to recognize the impact of their actions on their rivals and thus on the market as a whole.... When an industry contains one firm (monopoly) or many firms (pure competition), the individual sellers react only to impersonal market forces. In oligopoly they react to one another in a direct and personal fashion. This inevitable interaction of sellers in an oligopolistic market we call mutual interdependence. Where mutual interdependence exists, sellers do not just take into account the effects of their actions on the total markets ... they also take into account the effects of their actions on one another. Oligopoly becomes something like a poker game."[4]

It is a game in which the stakes are too high to engage in predatory price-cutting. This rule is so entrenched that oligopolists seldom break it. When they do – as in the case of the U.S. steel industry in 1982, or the tobacco industry in 1993 – the self-immolation is so painful that it doesn't take long for reason to return. Or, if it doesn't, pressure is likely to be applied by what John R. Munkirs calls the Central Planning Committee of the U.S. In his book *The Transformation of American Capitalism From Competitive Market Structures to Centralized Private Sector Planning*, Munkirs asserts that all of America's largest corporations are indirectly controlled and directed by seven large banks and five large insurance companies through a network of interlocking directorships representing either debt or equity interest in the company.[5] Heaven help any chief executive officer who pits his power against theirs.

Normally, oligopolists play according to their own tacitly understood set of rules and limit competition to advertising and promotion, style changes, and product improvement. This well-understood practice was confirmed for me some years ago by a senior executive of one of the big soap companies. At a luncheon following a seminar on the subject, one of his subordinates had been dutifully denying the remotest possibility of cooperation among companies. His chief, who didn't wish to appear ridiculous in the face of a convincing case, merely said, "Let's say we have an understanding."

Of course they do. Oligopolists do not write memoranda of agreement to set prices. They just reach an understanding over tea. Their costs rise at roughly the same rate, so their prices rise to about the same level at approximately the same time. That is quite natural and oligopolies are very good at doing what comes naturally.

LABOR

If the existence of natural monopolies and oligopolies chips away at the free-market illusion, the power and influence of the trade union movement undermine its very foundation. Combine the power of unions with that of oligopolistic and monopolistic employers and the whole concept of free-market price determination falls in ruins.

From the small, struggling craft unions the movement has grown to the point where it qualifies in its own right as big business. Not only do unions handle enormous sums of money for current operations, strike funds, and pensions, they exercise significant political clout. Even more important, from an economic point of view, big unions have become monopoly suppliers of labor in many of the big industries.

According to Harvard economists Richard Freeman and James Medoff, "Most, if not all, unions have monopoly power, which they can use to raise wages above competitive levels."[6] The power of unions to raise wages in excess of market levels is derived from privileges that have been extended by government through statutes, regulations and non-enforcement of other laws. In many jurisdictions it is an exceedingly powerful advantage. Ludwig von Mises, an economist who was not sympathetic to labor, wrote in 1922, "The long and short of trade union rights is in fact the right to proceed against the strikebreaker with primitive violence."[7] In some jurisdictions, that is no longer necessary because strike-breaking is prohibited by law and the only curb on a union's monopoly power is a threat by management to move the operation to a new locale or close it down altogether.

As a member of the Alliance of Canadian Cinema, Television and Radio Artists (ACTRA) I am not unfriendly to the legitimate aims and aspirations of labor. On the contrary! But as I told my good friend Shirley Carr, former president of the Canadian Labour Congress (Canada's equivalent to the U.S. AFL/CIO), being a union member doesn't take away my right to think. What is widely known as free collective bargaining can be, and often is, free collective blackmail and the results of its use are often detrimental to both the long-term interests of the workers involved and of their fellow citizens.

The consequences for the economy at large are monumental. Businesses are directly affected by the actions of their competitors. One generous settlement can create shock-waves for the whole industry, and it matters little whether the award is related to productivity or simply the vulnerability of the target company. It's a phenomenon that a number of economists, including Aubrey Jones, a former Tory cabinet minister, and later Wages and Prices Commissioner under a Labour government in the United Kingdom, have dubbed "wage leadership."[8] The most powerful union, in the most strategically advantageous position, sets the yardstick by which all subsequent negotiations are measured.

The practice is widespread in industrialized societies. *Wage Inflation and Wage Leadership: A Study of the Role of Key Wage Bargains in the Irish System of Collective Bargaining*, by W.E.J. McCarthy, J.F. O'Brien and V.G. Dowd, underlines its significance in that country. "One of the most important conclusions to emerge is that wage leadership could give rise to rapidly rising prices even if all other factors contributing to the latter process were totally neutralized. This is so because key wage claims, induced by disturbed relativities, can initiate a general upward movement in wage relativities. This vital point has never been explicitly brought out in the substantial body of statistical, economic and econometric work which has already been published concerning inflation in Ireland. The principal reason for this is that these disciplines cannot cope with the institutional dynamics which lie at the heart of the problem."[9]

That is the nut of it. The science of economics has no mathematical formula to quantify a phenomenon that is as much political and sociological as economic. A phenomenon, nevertheless, with incalculable economic consequences.

The impact from the unregulated exercise of monopoly union power has not yet been incorporated into the economic equation.   This results in some strange anomalies.   For example, natural monopolies have their prices to consumers regulated; yet one of their principal costs is not.   So wage increases, no matter how great, are just passed through to the consuming public.

I recall a former president of Bell Telephone of Canada – a monopoly at the time – vehemently insisting that big business was responsible enough to police its own labor settlements in a manner compatible with the public interest.   Only weeks later his company signed an extremely generous pace-setting agreement in order to avoid a strike.   Naturally, Bell was allowed to pass the highly inflationary cost increases on to its subscribers without penalty.   Not only that, the magnitude of the settlement became a benchmark for divers service unions.

In practice, oligopolies have often been pretty much in the same boat as monopolies – although that is certainly less so today than it was a decade ago.   To the extent that they have the collective market power to pass cost increases on to the consuming public, they are less responsible in policing their own settlements.   Like big labor, big business puts its own perceived short-term interests first.   Consequently, many contracts are signed that appear beneficial to business or labor or both but may be detrimental to the public interest.

Whether by monopolies, oligopolies or governments, it has been the approval of wage increases well in excess of average productivity that led inexorably to an ever higher-level of underlying inflation.   Each additional increase, whether in response to higher oil prices, more expensive food, or just a desire to keep up with a new record settlement, gave the spiral another twist.

WAGES OUT OF JOINT WITH PRODUCTIVITY

For more than a quarter of a century I have argued that the principal cause of contemporary inflation in Western industrialized economies is nominal wage increases being out-of-joint with productivity. Oil shocks and other price changes produce blips but the trend line is determined by the gap between nominal wages and real output.

Most economists recognize that there is a relationship between wages and prices. The President's Council of Economic Advisers was right on target in its 1981 report in saying: "... since payments to labor are estimated to account for almost two-thirds of total production costs, prices over the long term tend to move in conjunction with changes in labor unit costs."[10]

Precisely! In the longer term, prices move up at a rate that approximates the increase in wages and fringe benefits minus the increase in real output per person.

CONTEMPORARY INFLATION: $\dot{P} = \dot{W} - \dot{Q}$

The data support the proposition as closely as anything in economics. The rate of change in the price level will approximate the difference between the average rate of change in money wages, including fringe benefits, and the average rate of change in the production of goods and services. Stating this symbolically, we have $\dot{P} = \dot{W} - \dot{Q}$ where $\dot{P}$ is the rate of change in the price level, $\dot{W}$ is the average rate of change in money wages, and $\dot{Q}$ is the average rate of increase in real output of goods and services per worker in the labor force.

The assumptions include reasonable levels of employment. The definition varies from country to country, but for my purposes it is the condition that would be considered "normal" at the time. Another condition is a neutral monetary policy. This assumes that the money stock will be changed at a rate that will neither "overheat" nor "cool" the economy. The third assumption is that domestic prices are not unduly influenced by imports – that in fact import prices are rising at a rate more or less comparable to domestic prices.

Of course $\dot{P} = \dot{W} - \dot{Q}$ is an imprecise formula – especially in the short run – because its accuracy depends on assumptions that seldom apply for extended periods. But if one looks at the data for a group of fifteen O.E.C.D. (Organization for Economic Co-operation and Development) countries shown in Table 2 the long-term result for most countries is close. The over-all average of averages is amazingly accurate – within one-quarter of one percent over a 27 year period.[11] A correlation that close is very convincing!

TABLE 2

Average Growth Rates of Prices, Wages, and Productivity for 15 O.E.C.D. Countries
(W,Q calculated per member of the labor force), 1964-1991

	(1) P	(2) W	(3) Q	(4) W-Q	(5) (1)-(4)
Austria	4.3	7.7	3.0	4.7	-0.4
Belgium	5.0	7.7	2.5	5.2	-0.2
Canada	5.6	7.1	1.3	5.8	-0.2
Denmark	6.6	8.5	1.5	7.0	-0.4
France	6.3	9.2	2.5	6.6	-0.4
Germany	3.3	6.4	2.4	4.0	-0.6
Ireland	8.2	11.3	3.3	8.0	0.2
Italy	8.5	11.9	2.9	9.0	-0.6
Japan	5.2	9.5	4.4	5.1	0.1
Netherlands	4.6	6.3	1.5	4.8	-0.2
Norway	6.6	8.3	2.3	6.0	0.5
Sweden	6.9	8.9	1.7	7.2	-0.4
Switzerland	3.9	6.4	1.5	4.9	-1.0
U.K.	7.7	9.4	1.8	7.6	0.1
U.S.A.	5.2	6.0	0.8	5.2	0.0
Average	5.86	8.30	2.22	6.06	-0.20

Source:Q,W - OECD National Accounts; P=CPI in IMF
International Financial Statistics; Labor Force - OECD Labour Force Statistics.

It may be of interest to note that this is the fourth time I have had this table prepared for various periods beginning in 1958 and the correlation has always been of the same order of magnitude. The principal difference is that in the earlier post-war years wage settlements were lower, productivity was higher and consequently average inflation was much lower.

THE FATAL FLAW

The failure to recognize the primary role of wage increases in excess of productivity as the principal initiator of inflation since the system settled down after the Korean War has been the fatal flaw in economic theory and, by extension, public policy. Monetarists like Milton Friedman have recognized that the market for labor has been altered by legislation and regulation. In his book *Free to Choose*, where he discusses how the labor market operates, he says: "Here, too, interference by government, through minimum wages, for example, or trade unions, through restricting entry, may distort the information transmitted or may prevent individuals from freely acting on that information"[12]

Quite so! But having observed and objected to the rigidities in the labor market due to government intervention, he proceeds to ignore the connection between wages and prices by denying the existence of cost-push inflation. He pretends that the system is self-regulating and that equilibrium will be restored by some invisible hand. Yet even after two disastrous recessions and one inadequate recovery since *Free to Choose* was written the kind of free market he dreams of and writes about does not exist. Nor will it in his lifetime or mine.

The Friedman analysis of where capitalism went wrong and his conclusion that business cycles were caused by monetary excesses (too much or too little) is exactly what I believe. His concern that governmental intervention has reached the point where it actually impedes the satisfaction of human needs strikes a sympathetic cord and is consistent with my experience in the business world. But his solution to the problem of contemporary inflation is one that ignores the rigidities that he deplores. For him labor is just another price freely determined in the market.

This blind spot has been noted by many critics. In *Capitalism's Inflation and Unemployment Crisis*, Sidney Weintraub says: "To interpret money wages as 'simply another price' is to mistake flies for elephants." A general wage rise "comprises about 55 percent of gross business costs, closer to

75 percent of net costs, and probably even more of variable costs. "[13] In fact, money wages constitute the major factor in the economic equation; they far outshadow any other price.

In view of this, one should not underestimate the significance of Dr. Friedman's unsubstantiated contention that "wage increases in excess of increases in productivity are a result of inflation rather than the cause."[14] This proposition appears to fly in the face of the data. The Economic Report of the President 1995, shows that wages outstripped productivity in the United States every year from 1964 to 1994. Therein lies the principal source of the inflation for that period.

Not only have wages moved up faster than productivity, they outpaced prices in 18 of the 21 years prior to the time Milton and Rose Friedman first published *Free to Choose* in 1980 – the exceptions being '70, '74 and '79. The wage index for the entire 1964-1991 period has kept ahead of the price index. (See Figure 2)

U.S. Indices of Wages and Prices (1963-1994)

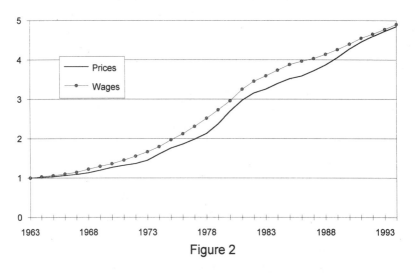

Figure 2

Source: IMF - *International Financial Statistics Yearbook*, 1993 and 1995

Disagreement concerning the origin of the wage-price spiral is exceeded only by apparent uncertainty as to which came first, the chicken or the egg. Businessmen know which came first.   Anyone who has made or sold a product or marketed a service knows that pricing begins by adding up the costs, including labor, and then adding a margin of profit. When the cost of labor rises faster than productivity, prices must rise. There are cases where a brisk demand may permit a higher markup or a slack demand may dictate a lower one; but inevitably the pricing mechanism begins by covering costs. Published data show that this is the sequence.

The following five graphs for the United States, Canada, Germany, the United Kingdom and Japan illustrate clearly that wages led prices almost exclusively. The few exceptions apply primarily in the United States and only after the monetarist counter-revolution had captured the hearts and minds of many theorists – which should provide them with scant solace. In fact price increases seldom if ever exceeded wage increases until stagflation became the dominant aspect of the system.   Then both business and labor were anticipating inflationary increases and attempts were made to leap-frog the process.

U.S. Wages and Prices (1956-1994)

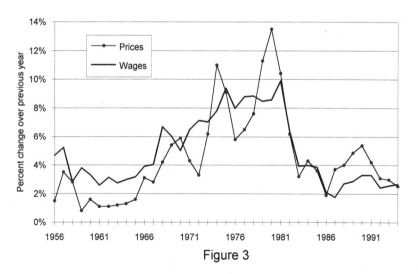

Figure 3

Source: IMF - *International Financial Statistics*, 1985 and 1995

Canadian Wages and Prices (1956-1994)

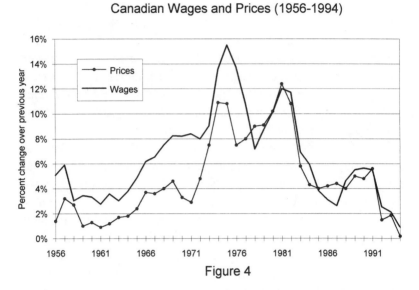

Figure 4

Source: IMF - *International Financial StatisticsYearbook*, 1985 and 1995

German Wages and Prices (1956-1994)

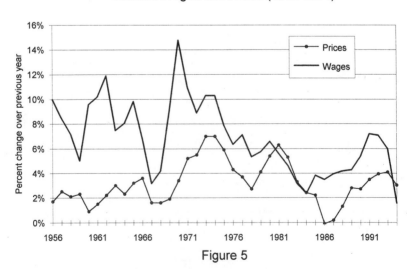

Figure 5

Source: IMF- *International Financial Statistics Yearbook*, 1985 and 1995

U. K. Wages and Prices (1956-1994)

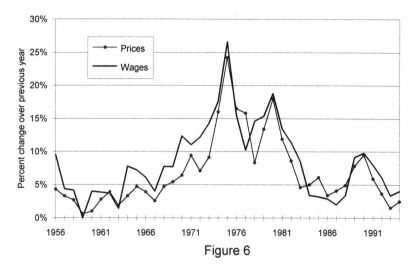

Figure 6

Source: IMF - *International Financial Statistics Yearbook* , 1985 and 1995

Japanese Wages and Prices (1956-1994)

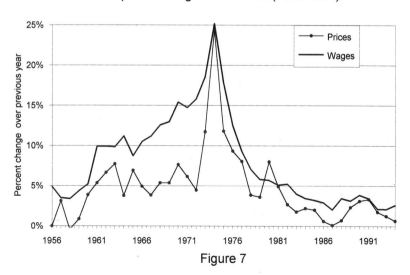

Figure 7

Source: IMF - *International Financial Statistics Yearbook* , 1985 and 1995

MONETARISM + MONOPOLY POWER = STAGFLATION

With both classical and monetarist economists either being unable to recognize or refusing to admit the predominant initiator of contemporary inflation, it is little wonder that official policy, based largely on their prescriptions, has been so disappointing at best and disastrous at worst. Attempts to control wage-push inflation by monetary means have been made at least six times since I first entered public life and always with the same results. The inflation rate has fallen but at the expense of employment and output. Eventually, when the rate of unemployment reached the political flash point, the monetary authorities have relaxed the system, lowered interest rates, and allowed the economy to expand and create more jobs. Each time the operation began the impression was given that the action taken would produce a permanent cure. But it never did! The end of one cycle simply marked the beginning of the next. It has for the last two decades, it does now and it will as long as the two protagonists – monetarists and monopoly power – are locked in combat.

CHAPTER 4

LIGHT ON THE HORIZON

*"Economics is the ecology of the human species ... the science
of the balance of human life and how it prospers or decays. "*

H.G. Wells

As soon as one is willing to accept the fact that the
principal generator of Western inflation since the Korean War
has been wages rising out of sync with productivity, the many
pieces of a complex jigsaw puzzle begin to fall into place. It
is obvious, in retrospect, that applying the monetary brakes in
1979, and from time to time since, resulted in increased unemployment and lower output. These two developments, in turn,
resulted in reduced revenues for governments while at the same
time increased the demand for government services. The reduced revenues led to larger deficits which had to be rolled over
into debt. The increased debt then compounded more quickly
due to the high interest rates encouraged by the Fed and other
central banks. Finally, the continuing effort to control inflation
by monetary means alone has resulted in projected growth rates
that are so low and real interest rates so high that the world
economy is set on a collision course with disaster.

A good starting point when considering a major change
in economic direction may be to consider what is desirable.
Long-standing goals have been high or "full employment", low

41

inflation, high growth rates and balanced federal, state and municipal budgets. The 64 trillion dollar question is the extent to which the desirable is compatible with the possible. Equally interesting is the correlation between the desirable and the "essential" necessary to "save" the system and prevent another horrendous crash.

To begin with there has to be a massive shift in perspective from short-term to long-term. All eyes seem to be glued to the ground. A small improvement in the unemployment figures and the stock market falls. A bit of bad news and the market recovers. Interest rates go up a bit and the bond market panics. A company has poor quarterly earnings and a manager is fired. No one seems to care that he might have been taking the long view. A country misses its budget deficit-cutting schedule and the manipulators of the massive pools of stateless hot money sell its bonds resulting in higher interest rates which slow down the economy and make it even more difficult to balance the budget. It's enough to make one dizzy. It is also all a little bit insane. So we have to lift our eyes to see where we are going, where we would like to go and where we must go for the benefit of the next generation.

FULL EMPLOYMENT

Full employment should be a top priority. People are more than cabbages. It should be a person's inalienable right to be able to work for a wage that will keep body and soul together. It is not just a question of economics, although most people prefer work to welfare; it is a matter of self-worth. There is something elevating about having a job and being able to contribute to the commonweal. It is good for the soul. So from a moral standpoint, full employment should be right up there with price stability.

What is full employment? I doubt that anyone has a magic number but on the basis of historical precedent, and for purposes of discussion, I am going to assume that it is about 4 percent unemployed for the United States. That is not as low as some countries have achieved, but it is a lot better than the

6 percent nonaccelerating inflation rate of unemployment (NAIRU) which too many economists and policy-makers have adopted as their moral law. I find it ironic that there were no such terms as the "natural rate of unemployment" or "non-accelerating inflation rate of unemployment" when I was young. These are just terms invented by economists to cover up the mysteries inherent in the monetarist counter-revolution.

A definition of full employment that I have always liked, and considered appropriate, is a rough equality between the number of job seekers and job openings. That means that job seekers might not be able to find the kind of job that they want, in the location that they prefer, but that they could find some kind of a job at some location and have the opportunity to put a foot firmly on the economic ladder which they hope to climb.

BALANCED BUDGETS

For people unable or unwilling to subscribe to the concept of full employment as a moral imperative let's take a look at the economics. There appears to be a correlation between unemployment and federal deficits. If you take a look at Figure 8 (next page) you will see that, generally speaking, when unemployment is low federal deficits are low or budgets balanced. When unemployment is high the federal deficit is much higher. Since 1949 there is only one case of a balanced budget when unemployment was significantly higher than 4%.

I doubt there is any mathematical formula on this score but one cannot ignore the aspect of common sense. When an additional 2 percent of the labor force are working and paying taxes government revenues rise. At the same time they require fewer handouts so government expenditures are reduced. With higher revenues and lower expenditures budgets move toward balance. The logic makes one wonder if Congress is pursuing the course of wisdom by attempting to balance the budget by cost-cutting measures alone. The cuts result in a loss of income for someone – a loss of income that will slow economic growth even more. In an economy already suffering from insufficient purchasing power (aggregate demand, as the economists call it) to buy all of the goods and services being offered (to clear the market) at existing prices, it is difficult to understand how a further reduction in incomes and consequently purchasing power will solve the long-term problems.

U.S. Unemployment and Deficits (1946-1994)

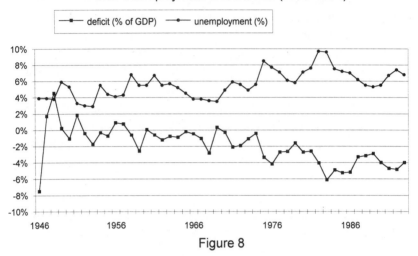

Figure 8

Source: *Economic Report of the President*, 1978 and 1995

HIGH GROWTH RATE

The U.S. slow growth rate is a big problem and one that is beginning to attract some attention. There is a desire to put the U.S. back on the fast growth track – say 3.5 percent instead of 2.3 to 2.5 percent – a hope which is shared by left and right alike. Both realize that it is the key to affluence. Both instinctively know that a higher growth rate would bring benefits at all levels. The difference arises when it comes to means. The *Wall Street Journal*, for example, in its lead editorial entitled "Across the Great Divide", on October 2, 1995, rejected pumping funds at social infrastructure, as recommended by Jeffrey Madrick in his book, *The End of Affluence*, while also disagreeing with the National Association of Manufacturers that an easier Fed might help.[1] If neither of these time honored remedies, what then?

The *Wall Street Journal's* opposition to an easier Fed is encrusted in the conventional wisdom of the moment. Escaping from that straight-jacket, as I have already pointed out, is a pre-requisite to getting the U.S. economy off what the *Journal* calls "its 2.5 percent leash." This intellectual leap is not optional if the system is to survive intact. Lower interest rates are not a luxury; they are absolutely essential to any kind of a cap on the debt burden (the ratio of total debt to GDP).

INTEREST RATES

In the last 12 months I have read more than a dozen editorials and financial columns warning of the dangers of low interest rates. Each author opined, in his or her own way, that lower interest rates would stimulate the economy, overheat it, and lead to renewed inflation – presumably on the scale of the 1970s. To the best of my knowledge I have seen no editorials or columns warning that high interest rates will allow the total debt to compound so fast that the economic ship will sink to the bottom of the sea.

In order to gain the perspective needed to contemplate the future one has to look back at Figure 1 (page 10) to be reminded that the ratio of total debt to GDP was more or less stable at around 140% of GDP from 1951, when some of the wartime debt had been retired, through until 1981 when the Fed pushed interest rates through the roof. The only reason that was possible, given our monetary system, is that average interest rates were not too far out of line with average growth rates. The near equality permitted stability in the ratio of debt to output.

So it isn't a question of "wouldn't it be nice?" to have lower interest rates. They are an absolute requirement for future stability. The trick is how to have consistently low interest rates without fear of fanning the inflationary embers.

LOW INFLATION

The fact that I listed full employment as my first priority

on moral (and economic) grounds should not mislead the right into thinking that I don't care about inflation. I do care for both moral and economic reasons. Let me quote from a little paperback called *Exit Inflation* that was published in 1981. In it I said: "Inflation is an insidious disease. Once it gets into the economic bloodstream it spreads quickly and soon gets out of control. Like most viruses, however, it affects some individuals more than others. We are not equally endowed with antibodies. The strong and the robust are relatively immune, while the old and the weak are alarmingly vulnerable."[2]

I not only stated the objection to inflation, which I consider a form of larceny, and the necessity of stamping it out, but went on to explain how a simple incomes policy directed at the root of the problem, the monopoly power of big business and big labor, would wrestle inflation to the ground without wrecking the economy in the process. A twelve month wage-price freeze would have reduced the double-digit inflation rate to near zero in one year and "inflationary expectations" with it. Once the inflation genie was back in the bottle the imposition of mandatory guidelines to limit the monopoly power of big business and big labor would have kept inflation in the 0-1 percent range, while permitting high growth and full employment at the same time. Needless to say low interest rates would have been possible and today's debt crisis would not have occurred.

To test the hypothesis for the Canadian scene econometric simulations were run for the period 1978-1985. Despite the most conservative of assumptions the benefits were enormous. Inflation would have been held to a very low level; there would have been 870,000 additional jobs in 1985; and the debts of governments (federal and provincial) would have been $50 billion to $82 billion less depending on the assumptions concerning appreciation of the Canadian dollar versus the United States dollar. For technical reasons the tests could not be extended beyond eight years but the economists involved estimated that had it been possible the debts of governments, by 1992, would have been $220 billion less.[3] The saving would have been even greater by 1995.

In view of the fact that the U.S. economy is roughly ten times the size of Canada's it is not unreasonable to assume that several million more jobs would have been available and that the federal debt would now be at least $2 trillion less, at the very minimum. But this essay is supposed to be about the future, rather than the past, so simulations have been run to show what might be possible if an incomes policy along the lines recommended in Chapter 10 were adopted in the U.S. now. The results are quite striking. Direct comparisons are made between the reference case, which represents an average projection of selected U.S. economists, and the results projected as a result of the incomes policy.[4]

Year	1996	1997	1998	1999
Gross Domestic Product (% change)				
Reference Case	2.2	2.0	2.0	2.7
Incomes Policy	2.2	2.9	3.6	3.1
Housing Starts (000's)				
Reference Case	1358	1312	1240	1249
Incomes Policy	1383	1457	1375	1257
Compensation per Hour (% change)				
Reference Case	3.9	3.8	3.5	3.2
Incomes Policy	2.0	1.1	1.7	1.9
Unit Labor Costs (non-farm)(% change)				
Reference Case	2.6	2.7	2.1	1.5
Incomes Policy	0.8	-0.5	-0.2	0.2
Consumer Price Index (% change)				
Reference Case	3.1	3.3	2.6	2.2
Incomes Policy	2.4	0.9	0.6	1.0
Prime Rate (%)				
Reference Case	9.00	8.62	7.69	7.50
Incomes Policy	8.30	6.29	5.61	6.27
Federal Funds Rate (%)				
Reference Case	6.01	5.61	4.62	4.40
Incomes Policy	5.20	3.10	2.55	3.20

While one has to be somewhat skeptical of econometric simulations, especially when they have misled the Fed so often over the years, they are useful for observing trend lines on the basis of different assumptions. In this case the results are numbers compatible with common sense. Smaller nominal wage increases result in lower labor unit costs. Lower labor unit costs result in significantly lower inflation, and the virtual elimination of inflationary expectations, allowing the Fed to reduce interest rates; lower interest rates stimulate the economy and result in higher growth and more jobs.

Had an incomes policy directed exclusively at monopoly power been introduced prior to the 1981-82 recession the system would probably have been able to muddle along for another 30 or 40 years without the kind of crises we have seen in the last 15 years and are likely to experience again in the future. Now, however, the big debt load, the very high leverage of the banking system, financial deregulation and the vast accumulation of hot money – national, international and stateless – has made the system so unstable that more heroic measures are required. It's time to take a fresh look at the 200 year-old debate about the monetary system and how it just grew like topsy.

MONETARY REFORM

Any systematic reading of post-industrial-revolution monetary history should lead one to the conclusion that the leverage of the banking system has been the principal cause of the booms and busts that have plagued Western capitalism in the 19th and 20th centuries. When we were on the gold standard, gold was the villain. Gold flowing into a country in payment for exports resulted in a rapid expansion of bank credit followed, almost inevitably, in a surge of economic activity leading to inflated prices. On the other side of the coin when gold left the country to pay for imports bank credit had to be curtailed. Economic activity slowed and recession or depression followed.

The system has changed very little since the abandonment of the gold standard and the substitution of cash reserves (or equivalent) for gold reserves as the fulcrum on which the banking system balances. Printing a dollar is not just a dollar if banks can use it to create an additional 20 or 30 dollars in credit. Similarly when a dollar is withdrawn from circulation the banking system has to reduce its outstanding loans by 20 or 30 dollars. Such high leverage not only puts the banking system in jeopardy, when it makes large bad loans as it did to Third World countries and also in overheated real-estate, it makes it extremely difficult to add monetary gas to the system smoothly enough to avoid cyclic fluctuations in output which are far greater than changes in the physical potential of the real economy would dictate.

U.S. Federal Reserve Discount Rate (1929-1994)

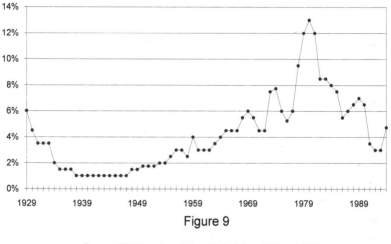

Figure 9

Source: IMF *International Financial Statistics*, 1984 and 1995,
U.S. Historical Statistics, 1976
(Note: annual highs to 1954, end of period value thereafter)

A look at Figure 9 indicates that in its attempt to regulate the money supply the Fed flies like a novice pilot. First it's nose up until the economy almost stalls, then it's nose down and hang on to your seat belts as the acceleration takes your breath away. A "soft landing" is currently the jargon of the street but very little is said about the advantage of straight and level flight. One could argue that all that is required is for the Fed to learn to fly but based on its record to date it would take a lot of instruction. Meanwhile reluctant passengers get a very bumpy ride.

Much of the apparent clumsiness is due to the high leverage of the monetary system. But in addition to the rough ride there is another problem that is seldom discussed in polite circles, that is, the connection between the banking system and debt. If you want to embarrass your banker ask him who creates the money to pay the interest on the money you have borrowed from him. The answer should be interesting if not particularly revealing.

If the private banking system creates nearly all the new money that is created each year, which is a fact, and all of the money created by the banks is created as debt and subject to interest, which is a fact, and no one creates any money with which to pay the interest, what does one have to do? The answer: one has to borrow more money with which to pay the interest on what one already owes and go deeper and deeper into debt in the process. This should provide a hint as to why all industrialized countries are so deeply in debt. It should also sound a warning that when debt compounds faster than new wealth is created, which is presently the case, there is trouble on the horizon.

Very radical changes are required to restore stability to the system. These changes cannot be effected by the financial community, including central banks, because they are vested interests. The changes can only be put into effect by courageous legislators willing to put the interests of the next generation ahead of other considerations. The greatest impediment to action in this area, however, is likely to be a lack of understanding of the problem. If the Congress is representative of the population at large, it is unlikely that more than a handful of members have a good working knowledge of the monetary system and the restrictions it imposes on public policy. For everyone who is interested, a little primer on the subject of money may be helpful.

CHAPTER 5

MONEY, FUNNY MONEY AND PHANTOM MONEY

"A national debt, if it is not excessive, will be to us a national blessing."

Alexander Hamilton

Where do babies come from? I can still remember some childhood discussions on the subject and some of the vague and inconclusive answers that were bandied about. Babies were found in cabbage patches. On other occasions it was a stork that brought them, though the connection between storks and cabbage patches was never too precise. By the time we reached puberty most of us knew that mummys' tummies had something to do with the wondrous process.

Those nebulous views belonged to the pre-television age. Today ten-year olds can get a pretty good sense of it all by watching Murphy Brown on TV. Other programs have actually shown live births which leave nothing to the imagination. You might expect, then, that most people would be equally well informed about where money comes from. Alas, that is not the case.

In the course of writing this book I asked scores of friends and associates – not including my circle of economist friends who are well versed in the subject – if they knew where money comes from. The sample included people with BAs,

MAs, PhDs, DDs, BScs, MScs, and lots of ordinary 'folk' with vast experience and much common sense. Not one of them had what I would call a working knowledge of the subject. Even more surprising, this was true of some who write columns and editorials on the subjects of money and economics in order to inform (or misinform) their readers about preferred priorities in public policy. Consequently, this chapter and the next will attempt to expose readers to at least a rudimentary knowledge of what money is and where it comes from. It is time that we removed the veil separating us from the financial holy of holies and see what the high priests of monetary orthodoxy do back there.

What is money? It is a good question for which there is no easy answer! It has meant different things to different people in different cultures in different times. Its importance was recognized in the Bible which refers to money more than seventy times. In those days money usually meant copper, silver or gold coins. An exception, and one of the earliest recorded examples of a breakdown in the monetary system, occurred during the seven-year famine recorded in Genesis. As Pharaoh's administrator, Joseph had accumulated all the money in both Egypt and Canaan in exchange for grain. But the people were still hungry so they came to Joseph and said, "Give us bread, for why should we die in your presence? For the money has failed." Joseph agreed to give them bread in exchange for livestock which became a substitute for money – an early example of mobile, liquid capital.[1]

A dual system of metallic coins and barter acted as the principal financial instruments worldwide for centuries. The first deviation from this appears to have occurred in China where they invented fei-ch'ien (flying money) which they used in a way similar to our bank drafts to send money from one place to another during the T'ang dynasty (A.D. 618-907). Later, when iron coins were the main currency in Szechwan province, the heavy weight led people to deposit them in some proto-banks and use the receipts for financial transactions. Many historians believe that the use of these receipts as a money substitute was the origin of paper money.[2]

For the next two centuries, through changing empires and dynasties, metal money coexisted with paper which had not yet become a national currency. In 1161, a new kind of money, the hui-tzu, or "check medium" was issued. It was tightly tied to reserves of copper coins so the exchange rate was kept constant for more than 20 years and it became a truly national currency around the end of the twelfth century. Then, in a situation that has been repeated innumerable times since, the government resorted to an inflationary policy of printing money to finance two wars. The inflation beginning in the second half of the twelfth century has been recorded as the first nationwide inflation of paper money in world history.[3]

THE GOLDSMITHS' SCAM

Although European banking can be traced back to Roman times my launching point is the introduction of paper money to England which appears to have begun with the London goldsmiths in the latter half of the 17th century. Until 1640 it was the custom for wealthy merchants to deposit their excess cash – gold and silver – in the Mint of the Tower of London for safe-keeping. In that year Charles I seized the privately owned money and destroyed the Mint's reputation as a safe place. This action forced merchants and traders to seek alternatives and, subsequently, to store their excess money with the goldsmiths of Lombard Street who had already built strong, fire-proof boxes for the storage of their own valuables.[4]

The goldsmiths accepted gold deposits for which they issued receipts which were redeemable on demand. These receipts were passed from hand to hand and were known as goldsmiths notes, the predecessors of banknotes. The goldsmiths paid interest of 5 percent on their customers' deposits and then lent the money to their more needy customers at exorbitant rates becoming, in fact, pawnbrokers who advanced money against the collateral of valuable property.[5] They also learned that it was possible to make loans in excess of the gold actually held in their vaults because only a small fraction of their depositors attempted to convert their receipts into gold.

Thus began the fractional reserve system, the practice of lending "money" that doesn't really exist. It was to become the most profitable scam in the history of mankind. It was also the quick-sand on which the Bank of England was subsequently founded in 1694 – just over three hundred years ago.

THE BANK OF ENGLAND'S SCAM

The Bank of England was conceived as a solution to a dilemma. King William's War, 1688-1697, had been extremely costly and this resulted in much of England's gold and silver going to the continent in payment of debt. As a result the money supply was sorely depleted and something had to be done to keep the wheels of commerce turning. Someone got the bright idea that establishing a bank might help to fill the void.

At the time the Bank was chartered the scheme involved an initial subscription by its shareholders of £1,200,000 in gold and silver which would be lent to the government at 8 percent. That seems fair enough, although the interest rate was more than ample for a government-guaranteed investment. It was only the beginning, however, because in addition to a £4,000 management fee, the Bank of England was granted an advantage only available to banks and bankers. It was granted authority to issue "banknotes" in an amount equal to its capital and lend the notes into circulation. This was not the first case of paper money issued by private banks in the modern era but it was the first of great and lasting significance in the English-speaking world.[6]

It was the same system developed by the goldsmiths. By lending the same money twice the Bank could double the interest received on its capital. Nice work if you can get it and you can with a bank charter. It is not too surprising, then, that discussions of this advantage encouraged some members of parliament to become shareholders in the Bank. Money lenders learned early, and have never forgotten, that it pays to have friends in parliament.[7]

The first Bank of England banknotes lent into circulation were, in fact, phantom money – the precursor of credit "money" which is very different from real money or legal tender. Public acceptance of the banknotes was based on the assumption that they were "as good as gold". Even when the Bank was subsequently authorized to increase the number of banknotes outstanding in proportion to the gold in its vaults the public seemed blithely unaware that the promise "to redeem in gold" was really a sham. The bankers got away with the deception because they knew, like the goldsmiths before them, that only a small fraction of banknote holders would attempt to redeem those notes at any one time. What had begun as a fraud had been legalized and legitimized, but that wasn't enough to protect the beneficiaries from the consequences of their own greed.

There were times when the Bank of England did not have enough gold in reserve to meet the day-to-day demands for conversion and within two years of operation an early "run" on the bank forced it to suspend payments in specie, that is, in coins as opposed to paper.[8] This was a situation that was to recur periodically through the next three centuries every time a "crisis" occurred as a result of a pressing need to increase the money supply at a rate in excess of the increase in gold and silver reserves, or when banks got too greedy and put credibility to the test.

"By the year 1725 all the basic essentials of the modern financial mechanism were in being" in England.[9] The Bank had increased its capital, its loans to the government, its issues of banknotes, and its "fractional reserves" for redeeming banknotes on demand, that is, the amount of gold the bank kept as a reserve, this being a small fraction of its outstanding banknotes. Most of the start-up problems of the bank had been disposed of and its status as a going concern firmly established. The Bank of England's unique charter gave it a virtual monopoly on banking in London.

This was not the case in other areas. By 1750 there were 12 banks outside London, and this number increased to 150 by 1776, and 721 by 1810.[10] These were called "country banks" and often they kept their reserves in banknotes of the

Bank of England, rather than in gold or silver coins or ingots. "As late as 1826 it was possible for Lord Liverpool to say that the law permitted any shopkeeper, however limited his means, to establish a bank ... and issue banknotes purporting to be payable on demand" in Bank of England notes that were, in turn, payable by the bank in specie on demand.[11] This was a classic example of paper money backed by other paper money – in essence phantom money guaranteed by phantom money.

Meanwhile on the other side of the Atlantic Ocean both French and English colonies encountered money supply problems and had to innovate as best possible. The French government neglected to meet the monetary needs of New France, as part of Canada was then known, and it was impossible to balance the budget with its heavy naval and military expenditures. Inflation began in 1685 when Intendant de Meulles, in great need of funds, cut playing-cards in four and signed them to serve as cash, and this card money increased in volume.[12]

GOVERNMENT-CREATED MONEY

The English colonial settlers faced comparable problems. Few were independently wealthy and the colonies suffered a chronic and often acute shortage of gold and silver coins. To make matters worse, Britain routinely banned the export of silver and gold to the colonies because it was desperately required as a base for the expansion of the money supply in the mother country. Deprived of support from "mother" England, necessity became the mother of invention.[13]

In 1690, four years before the Bank of England was chartered, the Massachusetts Bay Colony issued its first colonial notes. This, according to one of my American friends, was a consequence of their part in King William's war. Soldiers had been dispatched to invade Canada on the promise that the French had lots of silver, "Beat 'em and get paid that way", is how he told the story. But Quebec did not fall and the Yanks went back to Boston sore, mean, and unpaid. Something had to be done, so the Massachusetts Bay Note, redeemable in gold "sometime", was born. "This was, if not the very first, one of the first cases of government-created paper money of the modern age."[14]

Early in the 18th century, in May 1723, Pennsylvania loaned into circulation, with real-estate as security, notes to the amount of £15,000; and another £30,000 was issued in December. It was enacted that, "counterfeiters were to be punished by having both their 'ears cut off', being whipped on the 'bare back with thirty lashes well laid on,' and fined or sold into servitude."[15] While the punishment for counterfeiters seems somewhat extreme by 20th century standards, the issue of notes accomplished its purpose and sparked a revival of the colony's economy. Ship-building prospered and both exports and imports increased markedly.[16]

The experiment was so successful that the number of notes in circulation was increased from £15,000 in early 1723, to £81,500 in 1754 – a growth rate during the thirty-one years of a moderate 5.6 percent. Even Adam Smith, who was not a fan of government-created money, admitted that Pennsylvania's paper currency "is said never to have sunk below the value of the gold and silver which was current in the colony before the first issue of paper money."[17]

As I mentioned at the outset, the Chinese had used paper money centuries earlier, but for our part of the world, as Curtis P. Nettles points out: "Paper currency issued under government auspices originated in the thirteen colonies; and during the 18th century they were the laboratories in which many currency experiments were performed."[18] There were no banks at that time in any of the 13 colonies so all the paper money was created under the authority of the colonial legislatures. In all there were about 250 separate issues of colonial notes between 1690 and 1775 and the system worked just fine when they avoided over or under issue. It also had distinct advantages over bank or coin money. The legislature could spend, lend or transfer the money into circulation, while banks could only lend (or spend their interest earnings back into circulation) and the coin money was always leaving the colonies to pay for imports.

There is no doubt that the 13 colonies were the Western pioneers in the creation of "funny money", the label many skeptics and cynics apply to government-created money. Why they consider it any funnier than the phantom money banks create I will never understand. Perhaps they just suffer from a peculiar sense of humor.

Historians usually play down the role of money creation as a causal factor in bringing about the War for Independence. On the other hand, "[Benjamin] Franklin cited restrictions upon paper money as one of the main reasons for the alienation of the American provinces from the mother country."[19] "To a significant extent, the war was fought over the right of the Colonists to create their own money supply. When the Continental Congress and the states brought forth large issues of their own legal-tender money in 1775, they committed acts so contrary to British laws governing the colonies and so contemptuous and insulting to British sovereignty as to make war inevitable."[20]

When the war began the United Colonies, or the United States, as they came to be called, were really strapped for gold and silver. Their difficulty was compounded by the blockade imposed by the British Navy. At the same time the war had to be financed by one means or another so the separate states, and the United States, acting through the Continental Congress in an act of defiance against King and parliament, continued the policy that they had previously followed when gold was in short supply – they issued paper money. But now there was a difference. Instead of just printing enough to meet the needs of a moderate growth in trade they had to print an amount which, when added to foreign borrowing and the receipts from taxation, was sufficient to finance the war. Inevitably that amount ceased to have any relation to the increase in output of goods and services and the paper began to lose its value. In 1784 Benjamin Franklin, after defending the necessity of what was done, went on to explain the consequences of excess. "It has been long and often observed, that when the current money of a country is augmented beyond the occasions for money as a medium of commerce, its value as money diminishes...."[21]

It is a truism to which one can say Amen! The amount of money created was so great that its worthlessness was inevitable.

It is noteworthy, however, that much of the hyper-inflation of the later years of the Revolution was caused by British counterfeiting in a deliberate attempt to discredit the Continental currency. If that was their aim they succeeded brilliantly but in this particular round of the war over money it was the colonies that had the last laugh. They paid for much of their war effort by issuing "funny" money and the total cost, including interest, until the debt was liquidated, has been estimated as about $250 million. Britain, on the other hand, relied almost entirely on "phantom" bank-created borrowed money. By 1783, the British national debt was roughly $500 million greater than in 1774. But here is the really interesting fact: Britain's national debt has never since 1783 been less than it was at the end of that year. The conclusion that William Hixson draws in his excellent book the *Triumph of the Bankers* (which should be required reading for every student of monetary policy) is that "Britain has not even yet finished paying for the war it lost attempting to suppress the emerging United States."[22] Hixson goes on to say that in the intervening 200 years British taxpayers have paid over $4 billion in interest to their moneylending class of 1783 and its heirs. To add injury to insult, the original $500 million is still outstanding.[23]

While the Americans won that round, future historians may speculate about who "lost" the next one. As a result of the hyperinflation, and the discredited "Continental", Alexander Hamilton, who seemed determined to model the United States monetary and banking system on that of England, was able to get a federal charter for the first Bank of the United States (BUS) and several state banks were chartered. This despite the strongly expressed views of Benjamin Franklin, John Adams and Thomas Jefferson. The Jeffersonians hated the BUS and had it killed after 20 years. Meanwhile the United States didn't create any legal tender paper money from the Revolution until Lincoln's Greenbacks, but this over-reaction exacted a heavy price.

The years immediately following the War for Independence were not happy ones for the people of the United States. The collapse of the monetary system, and the absence of sufficient gold and silver to facilitate trade, caused the country to experience its first great depression. Debtors who had been able to pay creditors with cheap money during the inflationary period now had to pay with money that was scarce and therefore dear. Thus, as Richard B. Morris explains, "each one of the thirteen states found creditors arrayed against debtors."[24] The depression constituted the second half of the lesson in monetary theory. Whereas too much money leads to inflation, too little leads to economic paralysis. Unfortunately these inalienable truths proved to be an insufficient guide for future policy makers.

For almost a century following the War for Independence arguments about "money questions" and the role of banks raged on. Myriad new state banks appeared but when the United States declared war on Britain on June 18, 1812, the task of financing the conflict was considerably more difficult due to the absence of any sort of "central bank". Gold had to be exported to pay for armaments and hoarding was rampant; so except for a few banks in New England most were forced to suspend redemption of their notes on demand, and convertibility was not re-instated until February 1817.[25]

Meanwhile the banking industry was not unaware of the opportunity this presented on the financial side of the economy. The number of banks in the U.S. increased from thirty, in 1800, to seven hundred and thirteen by 1836. By then they had created $306 million in banknotes, plus deposits, but had only about $40 million in gold in their vaults. The ratio for the banks total liabilities – bank notes plus deposits – to metallic reserves was just about seven and a half to one.[26]

Although regulation of the banks was inadequate or non-existent some banks followed very conservative reserve policies. Others, however, did not! An extreme example is provided by the Farmers' Exchange Bank of Gloucester (Rhode Island), founded in 1804. An investigating committee of the state legislature found that on the basis of only $3 million capital stock in gold, by 1809 the bank had loaned into circulation banknotes it had itself created to the total amount of $580 million.   In other words it had only sufficient reserves to liquidate about half a cent for every dollar of its obligations.[27]

It was the Civil War, however, which had the biggest impact on the system.   Once again gold was in short supply so the banks suspended payment, making the issue of United States Notes [greenbacks] unavoidable.   Although the need was to meet the exigencies of war there had long been a need for a "universal" or national currency to replace the hodgepodge existing at the time.   One historian estimated that in 1860 there were "7,000 kinds of paper notes in circulation, not to mention 5,000 counterfeit issues."[28]

VICTORY OF THE BANKERS

From the time greenbacks first came into circulation in 1862 they carried the words: "The United States of America will pay to the bearer five dollars ... payable at the United States Treasury."   In fact, however, they were government-created inconvertible money until 1879 when they first became convertible into gold at face value.   Convertibility was introduced by Hugh McCulloch, a former banker and gold monometallist who became secretary of the treasury in 1865. He agreed with his old buddies in the banking fraternity that steps should be taken to make greenbacks convertible into gold as soon as possible.

Since there were hundreds of millions of dollars in paper outstanding at the time, and little gold in the treasury with which to redeem it, McCulloch concluded that it would be easier to reduce the number of greenbacks than to increase the gold in the treasury.   So he sold bonds in exchange for greenbacks and then destroyed the greenbacks.   In other words he exchanged interest-bearing debt for non-interest-bearing debt.[29]   It is interesting to speculate what might have happened had McCulloch been a farmer or businessman.   In any event, he decided to emulate mother England by putting the country in debt.   There is little doubt that it was the bankers and moneylenders who won that round.

THE GOLD STANDARD – ANOTHER WRONG TURN

Of the three categories of monetary enthusiasts, those who preferred gold-backed currency, those who were quite willing to settle for silver-backed, and those who preferred no metal backing at all, it was ultimately the monometallists or gold standard supporters who carried the day. The gold standard was a commitment by participating countries to fix the prices of their domestic currencies in terms of a specific amount of gold – a practice followed in various European countries from time to time. "England adopted a de facto gold standard in 1717 ... and formally adopted the gold standard in 1819."[30] Convertibility was suspended during the Napoleonic War and re-instated in 1821, at the urging of economist David Ricardo, and others, at the pre-war rate of exchange.

"The United States, though formally on a bimetallic (gold and silver) standard switched to gold de facto in 1834 and de jure in 1900. Other major countries joined the gold standard in the 1870s. The period from 1880 to 1914 is known as the classical gold standard."[31] Eventually it became an international standard though it had to be abandoned during wartime as a matter of expediency. Later, when economic activity returned to normal, there was always pressure for its re-instatement.

The classical attachment to the gold standard was so strong that even the redoubtable Winston Churchill was captive of its orthodoxy. As Chancellor of the Exchequer, he was largely responsible for England's return to the gold standard at the old parity after World War I. In his Budget speech of April 28, 1925, he declared that: "A return to the gold standard has long been a settled and declared policy of this country. Every Expert Conference since the war ... has urged in principle the return to the gold standard. No responsible authority has advocated any other policy."[32]

Churchill stressed that in addition to those countries that had already returned to the gold standard there should be simultaneous action by Holland, the Dutch East Indies, Australia and New Zealand. Some other countries used U.S. dollars or British pounds as reserves on the basis that those currencies were convertible into gold and consequently they could be considered an acceptable substitute for gold. Churchill described the advantage of this common international action in the following metaphor: "That standard [the gold standard] may of course vary in itself from time to time, but the position of all countries related to it will vary together like ships in a harbour whose gangways are joined and who rise and fall together with the tide."[33]

Churchill based his case primarily on the Report of the Committee on the Currency and Bank of England Note Issues. The arguments of the Committee were brief and clear as far as they went, although they were described as jejune (devoid of substance) by J.M. Keynes. They never explored the general desirability of a gold standard from the point of view of the interests of the different social classes affected by its operation. The general advantages of a gold standard were not stated by the report, but were taken for granted as self-evident. So much for the opinions of "experts".

In retrospect one wonders why support for the gold standard was so deeply entrenched. It was obvious that every time gold went out of the country the money supply contracted and this had a negative effect on the domestic economy. On the other hand when gold came into the country or new gold discoveries occurred the money supply increased rapidly and inflation took hold. This uncritical attachment to the gold standard must have had something to do with mysticism or its long romantic history as a prize worthy of kings and buccaneers. As an economic regulator, however, it was an abomination.

It is difficult for me to credit that such an absurd system would last until August 15, 1971, when President Richard Nixon announced that the United States would no longer redeem currency held by foreign central banks for gold. This action was the last gasp of the gold standard. It is even more difficult to believe, as Michael D. Bordo says in his essay on the Gold Standard in the *Encyclopedia of Economics*: "Widespread dissatisfaction with high inflation in the late seventies and early eighties brought renewed interest in the gold standard."[34] If true, and recent news reports confirm the fact, it only proves that some economists are incapable of learning.

To put the issue in perspective, just imagine that a group of visiting little green men and women from some other planet came to earth with a special laser gun which attacked only gold and caused it to disintegrate. In the course of their invasion they destroyed the entire gold supply on and in the earth. The effect on the real economy would be minimal. Jewellers would have to find substitutes for their brilliant wares and dentists would have to find something else to fill the gaping holes created in so many teeth. But apart from a few special cases, little would be affected. Our ability to grow food, in infinite variety, would not be changed. The potential for the production of bicycles, cars, ships and planes would not be affected. In other words we could cope quite nicely thank you. To say that without gold we would shut down the entire economy, or even slow it down dramatically, is too absurd for serious consideration. It should never have been the regulator of economic activity in industrialized economies.

It makes little difference to most of us how much gold our income will buy. What concerns us is the kind of "basket" of goods and services that Irving Fisher wrote about and which is now the basis for a consumer price index. How much food, clothing, and shelter will our pay-check buy and will there be anything left over for dinner out and family vacations? Also will it buy as much next year as it does now? And what about a few years from now, after we retire? These are the variables that we hope will be constant, on average, not how many gold or silver wafers we can buy with our dollars, pounds or marks. It is the package of goods and services that these currencies can be exchanged for which determines their value.

SUMMARY

To the question "what is money?", then, there is no single or simple answer. It has taken many forms over the centuries and new ones are being invented. Today most of the high quality coins of silver, gold and platinum are sold as collectors items. The day-to-day coins are usually alloys and, although they still form an essential part of the system, they really fall into the "small change" category. The fraction of the total value of transactions settled with coins is infinitesimal.

Paper money, or electronic impulses, now rule the day. We have gone through a history of paper money that was convertible, at least in theory, into gold; paper that was "backed" by silver; paper that was backed by other paper allegedly convertible into gold; and paper labeled "legal tender" backed by the authority of the state. In the final analysis money is anything that ordinary people will readily accept in exchange for their goods and services. That is not the end of the story, however; it is really just the beginning.

One of the most important lessons from history is that when the money supply is increased faster than the output of goods and services, prices rise. Too much money causes inflation and it doesn't matter whether it's gold-backed money, government-created money, or bank-created non-convertible credit money. As J.K. Galbraith points out in his book *Money, Whence it Came, Where it Went*, one of the worst inflations Europe saw was when gold and silver were imported in large quantities from the Americas.[35]

On the other side of the coin it is obvious that too little money has, historically, led to economic stagnation. Whenever the money supply was contracted, the economy grew at a rate below its potential or, in many cases, shrank. So money is more than just a determinant of prices as some monetarists claim. A shortage of purchasing power (aggregate demand), such as we saw during the great depression of the 1930s, and again in the two most recent and terrible recessions, slows an economy well below its potential, with the unhappy and sometimes tragic consequences which inevitably follow for individuals and families.

Finally, and fundamentally, it makes a profound difference how money is created. Government-created money is born free of encumbrance. **Bank-created credit money is slave money in the sense that it is brought into the world with a lien on it**. When the proportion of money created as debt is too great we find ourselves in the kind of Catch-22 we now face. To pay the interest on all that debt we have to borrow more and more all the time which is comparable to being in a deep hole and digging ourselves in deeper all the time.

CHAPTER 6

PHANTOM MONEY REIGNS SUPREME

"This is a pretty flim-flam."

Francis Beaumont and John Fletcher

Professor Joseph E. Stiglitz has written that banks "can be viewed as highly leveraged firms that borrow from depositors."[1] You better believe it – much too highly leveraged for the public good. Another definition which gives a better idea of what they actually do is this: "Banks are firms that borrow, lend, store, manufacture and destroy money." These are their principal functions although they are increasingly engaged in a number of other businesses where the legitimacy of their presence is open to question. It is their ability to create and destroy money, however, which provides the world's greatest economic challenge.

Those participants in the unofficial poll mentioned in the previous chapter who were willing to hazard a guess as to "where money comes from" invariably said, after some reflection, "the government prints it". When asked pointedly what proportion of new money they thought was printed by government the estimates ranged from 60 percent to 100 percent. There were no guesses below 60 percent which, for me, confirmed the belief that money and banking constitutes the greatest void in public understanding of how our economic system works and why it sometimes works less well than we would like. Governments, or central banks on their behalf, only print a small fraction of the total money supply, or money stock as it is often called. In the U.S., at the end of 1992, it was about 8% of the total. Nearly all new money is created in the form of credit by private banks licensed for that purpose.

MULTIPLE CREATION OF MONEY BY THE BANKING SYSTEM

A simplified version of the process goes something like this. When the Federal Reserve System (Fed) decides to increase the money stock it buys some government bonds, let's say a million dollars worth for purposes of illustration. It pays for them by issuing a check for a million dollars drawn on itself. This is the equivalent of cash and economists call it "high-powered money" because it is the kind of money banks can use as reserves in order to create a much larger amount of "deposit money". When we were on the gold standard, gold was considered high-powered money. Today, high-powered money consists of (1) paper money (cash) with "legal tender" printed on it and (2) private banks' deposits at the Fed.

Let's assume that the entire million of new cash winds up in the banking system, i.e. in bank vaults or in the banks' deposits with the Fed. They are then in a position to make new loans equal to several times the amount of fresh cash. Economist Anna J. Schwartz describes the process this way.

"If the required reserve ratio is 20 percent, then starting with new reserves of, say, $1,000, the most a bank can lend is $800, since it must keep $200 as reserves against the deposit it simultaneously sets up. When the borrower writes a check against this amount in his bank A, the payee deposits it in his bank B. Each new demand deposit that a bank receives creates an equal amount of new reserves. Bank B will now have additional reserves of $800 of which it must keep $160 in reserves, so it can lend out only $640. The total of new loans granted by the banking system as a whole in this example will be five times the initial amount of excess reserve, or $4,000: 800 + 640 + 512.40 + 409.60, and so on."[2] While this is an accurate portrayal of the process the reserve ratio of 20 percent is unrealistic.   Current reserve requirements for most bank deposits, as I will point out later, are 3% or less. So banks are likely to create $20,000 to $30,000 of new "money" for each $1,000 of additional reserves.

I think it is simpler for most of us to understand the phenomenon of bank-created money when we consider how many of us as individuals have been, or might be in the future, involved in the money-creation process. Let's assume that you would like to borrow $20,000 to buy a car or perhaps a new machine to make widgets in the basement. A visit to your friendly banker will set the ground rules. You will be told that you will have to provide collateral. If you have a drawer-full of stocks and bonds with market value well in excess of the amount to be borrowed that will probably be acceptable. If not, a mortgage on your house, assuming you have sufficient equity, may do. Failing that the personal guarantees of a couple of rich uncles or aunts might suffice.

Once the collateral has been agreed and deposited with the bank for safe-keeping, you will be asked to open an account and sign a note for the amount to be borrowed. Minutes later the bank will put $20,000 in your account and you can write a check any time you like. The important point is that just minutes earlier the $20,000 you have to spend didn't exist. It was created out of thin air based on nothing more than a small fractional reserve held by the bank.

An important point should be kept in mind, however. Although the bank "created" the $20,000 that was put in your account as a deposit this "phantom money" – or money equivalent as it's sometimes called – was created as debt. You still owe the bank $20,000 and you won't get your collateral back until you repay the loan in full with interest.

An even more striking illustration of how the system of new money-creation works is to consider someone in the building business who borrows $150,000 to build a house. This money is used to pay the people who dig clay from a pit and make bricks, the bricklayers who lay the bricks, the woodsmen who cut trees to make lumber, the carpenters who use it to build the frame, the miners who extract the metals for the hardware and the manufacturers who turn out the plumbing, wiring and fixtures. But when they are all finished it is the bank which owns the house. The bank did little more than create the "money" which acted as the intermediary to facilitate construction. Nevertheless, because it was created as debt, all of the money used to pay for the new house had a lien on it. Consequently the builder has to sell the house at a price that will allow him to repay the bank and, if he is lucky, leave a little over to reward him for the work he has done and the risk he has taken. If he can't, and there is a shortfall, he will have to make up the difference to prevent the bank from liquidating part or all of the collateral pledged to get the loan.

In reality, then, the banks have turned the world into one humongous pawn shop. You hock your stocks, bonds, house, business, rich mother-in-law or country and the bank(s) will give you a loan based on the value of the collateral. Still there is an element of uncertainty in dealing with the banks that doesn't apply with legitimate pawn shops. The latter don't phone you and ask for their money back if the price of gold or silver goes down after they have given you cash for your gold watch or silver candlesticks. The banks, on the other hand, often change the terms of the deal with little warning. If the market value of your collateral goes down, they phone and insist that you either provide additional collateral, which you may not have, or give them their "money" back which isn't always easy if too many banks are simultaneously insisting on the repayment of too much "money" (in cash) which doesn't really exist. In the case of loans to countries, the banks can't really foreclose so they just begin to act like owners and tell the political managers how they want "their" country run.

The banks are often referred to as financial intermediaries who take money from some people and lend it to others. It is a part truth but also part fiction when you consider that banks create more than 90% of the increase in the money stock each year in the form of debt and with less and less cash or reserves to back it up.

In view of this it was more than a little surprising that Anna J. Schwartz used a 20 percent reserve requirement in her *Encyclopedia of Economics* example when there hasn't been a reserve that high in heaven knows when. You will recall that when the Bank of England was first chartered in 1694, it was only allowed to lend its capital twice. Then some collusion between bankers and politicians relaxed the reserve requirement. In the United States, for federally chartered banks, the reserve requirement was 25% in the late nineteenth century but this was reduced about the time the Fed was established in 1913 and the slide has continued, periodically, ever since. On December 31, 1992 the Fed reserve requirement for Net transaction accounts (deposits against which you can make withdrawals or transfers) was 3 percent for the first 46.8 million and 10 percent for deposits in excess of that amount; 0 reserve was required against non-personal time deposits (savings); and 0 reserve against Eurocurrency liabilities.[3] The regulations are too complicated for mere mortals to understand but for anyone brave enough to try they are repeated in full in Appendix A. They are also too frightening for restful sleep. What they say to me is that the Fed and the banking industry have jiggered definitions in a way that permits excessive leverage.

Figure 10 (next page) demonstrates the results of the manipulation. Whereas in 1963 there was one real dollar, or reasonable facsimile, for every ten dollars you had in the bank, that is no longer the case. Today you may have 25 to 30 dollars "in the bank" against which only one legal tender dollar exists. This is obscene. Greed knows no bounds!

Other countries' rules are as bad or worse. In Germany, the Bundesbank has current reserve requirements (May '94) of 5% on call loans and 2% on term deposits and savings accounts. In the United Kingdom, institutions which are members of the U.K. banking sector, and which have reported eligible liabilities (ELs) averaging 10 million pounds or more, accept an obligation to hold non-operational, non-interest-bearing deposits (cash ratio deposits) with the Bank of

England. The level of an institution's cash ratio deposits is calculated twice a year, in April and October, as 0.35% of the average ELs reported. Compare that to the 50% when the Bank of England was first chartered as a private bank. In Canada the Bank Act of 1991 provided, unbelievably, for the total elimination of reserves over a two year period – a move that, thankfully, the U.S. has resisted so far. Canadian banks just keep the minimum amount of cash they expect their customers to withdraw from day-to-day.

U.S. Commercial Bank Leverage (1963-1994)

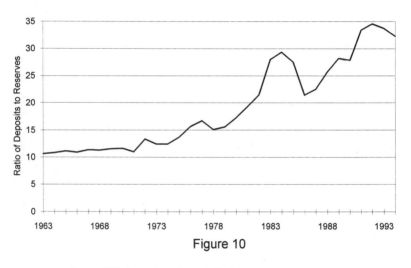

Figure 10

Source: IMF - *International Financial Statistics Yearbook*, 1993 and 1995
(See note 4)

To understand the effect of the banking system on the real economy it may be useful to think of the money stock as soup. In some Eastern European countries, and also in some Third World countries where there is little to buy, the soup is mostly water. But in the highly developed Western economies our soup is rich with tasty morsels of meat and an endless variety of vegetables representing the incredible spectrum of goods and services that are available in such abundance. In other words, if you have cash you can satisfy almost any need or want.

Each year the soup is watered when the banking system increases the money stock. As long as they don't dilute it too much the system can produce the extra meat and vegetables to maintain the same rich tantalizing consistency. Either too much or too little can have negative effects on the brew. In real life the amount of dilution which will maintain the same consistency is determined by the potential to increase the supply of goods and services. This depends on the natural growth in the labor force, net immigration and participation rates (the proportion of the total population which chooses to work), as well as the level of education and skill of the total labor force, coupled with the use of more and better machines. For two centuries output has tended upward when monetary conditions, the means of exchange, has allowed.

WHO GETS THE LOANS

How the banks have been ladling out the increase in money for the last decade or so has put the world on notice that things are not as they used to be. This is a matter of concern because monetary dilution affects everybody from the poorest beggar with a cupful of change through to the multi-billionaire. In the real world some are treated much more generously than others and to a very large extent the banks decide who the winners and losers will be. Giving them a near-monopoly on the creation of money, and then allowing them almost unrestricted liberty as to what they can do with it, can best be described as double jeopardy. The banks may not have invented the maxim "the rich get richer and the poor get poorer" but they certainly do their best to prove its validity by giving the lion's share of the increase to their friends, beginning with themselves. Get a breakdown, if you can, of the employee benefits hidden in the fine print within any bank annual statement and you will probably find a list of loans to executives for the purchase of homes or the acquisition of shares in the bank for which they have been given options. Often they get a preferred interest rate that makes even their best customers green with envy. They have another tremendous advantage in that when a loan comes due they can either renew it or give themselves large salary increases and bonuses sufficient to retire the loans. If only everyone were in such a privileged position.

Other people who have access to increases in the money supply fall into the general category of "those who don't need it". They are well-to-do people with collateral assets who can borrow money from the banks, buy shares or property in anticipation of an increase in value, deduct the interest on the loan from their taxable income and make themselves a tidy profit if they have anticipated market conditions correctly. It's nice work if you can do it but only people with collateral assets are in a position to take advantage of the opportunity and they are the people who need it the least.

The banks are equally generous with their favorite large businesses and often invite the CEO to be a member of their board. That can make a difference. Two of my friends in the development business went to every Canadian bank in 1993 in an effort to borrow money for a large Vancouver project, with an assured future, in which they were investing 50 percent of the total cost from their own resources. No bank would look at the loan until a director of their company, who was also a bank director, interceded on their behalf and the loan was granted.

The trend in banking throughout the 1980s and into the 1990s is alarming. Small business has been devastated, while billions have been made available for takeovers and leveraged buyouts. The most credit-worthy borrowers kept raising the ante as they tapped the banking system for giant ladles of newly-created soup for the purpose of buying up other people's businesses. The banks loved it because it is so much easier to clip one coupon rather than worry about a thousand different collections – only one or two balance sheets to read rather than a drawer-full. Even then there were balance sheets that were not adequately checked when the borrower was also a director of the bank.

The trend of the 1980s was summed in the following quotation from John Ralston Saul's book, *Voltaire's Bastards*:

"Capitalist creativity has been discouraged and financial manipulation encouraged. This starvation campaign has left the fat slightly thinner, having converted some of their flesh into cash. Now they are beefing themselves back up by picking over the carcasses of the young and lean. In 1984 alone, $140 billion was spent in the United States on mergers, acquisitions and leveraged buyouts. By 1988 this was almost $300 billion, with 3,310 companies involved.... The inevitable passing of the leveraged buyout as it first appeared does not represent a change in the situation, but rather the passing of a particular tool for speculation. For example, worldwide merger-acquisition transactions had risen to $375.9 billion in 1988, involving 5,634 deals. Then came the collapse in the speculative market. And yet the figures in 1989 were only marginally down, to $374.3 billion involving 5,222 deals."[5]

The number of questionable deals is staggering. One which was of particular interest to me was Robert Campeau's grandiose acquisitions. This was because I had known him as a builder and as a member of the Canadian *Task Force on Housing and Urban Development*, which I chaired. So, following his acquisition of Allied Stores, it was a matter of some amazement when he attempted to acquire Federated Department Stores' chain which comprised Bloomingdale's, Abraham & Strauss, Burdines, Lazarus, Rich's and Goldsmith's, amongst others. Actually I was more than somewhat dismayed because his expertise was in construction, where he had succeeded admirably; but he knew nothing about retailing, the amount of money involved was out of his league and I disapproved of anyone being able to borrow several billions to buy other people's businesses. Still he was able to borrow almost the entire purchase price from a dozen banks and a trio of brokerage houses – a fact which shook my confidence in the U.S. financial industry to the core.

If the 1980s broke previous records for merger-mania their place in history has now been usurped by the 1990s. Before the end of October, 1995, the Security Data Corporation reported that mergers and acquisitions for the year to date was near $346 billion, just shy of a record $347.1 billion in 1994.[6]

At the same time D. Scott Lindsay of CS First Boston estimated that worldwide mergers and acquisitions could reach $800 billion in '95 with a two year total of $1.3 trillion.[7]

According to Peter Schoenfeld, vice-chairman of Schroder Wertheim & Co., many combinations – particularly in the financial services and media industries – have been made possible partly because of technological and regulatory changes. He called officials in the U.S. Justice Department – who closely monitor mergers to ferret out any possible antitrust concerns – an "enlightened group of regulators. There is none of this 'bigness is bad' mentality that is floating around", he said.[8]

Perhaps, but there is no guarantee that bigness is good either. At a certain size, when oligopoly is achieved, new entrants are effectively denied access to the field. In addition, in a global economy, where does consolidation end? You can be very sure that there are companies in each industry, with virtually unlimited access to bank credit, which will be hell-bent for world hegemony. At a certain point the dominant company in each trading block will likely plead the case for monopoly in order to compete head to head with the biggest and fiercest in other trading blocks. At this point, not too many years hence, the regulators may look back on their benign neglect and wonder what kind of world they have created.

The common thread in all this madness is participation by the banks. Westinghouse Electric Corp. signed loan agreements of $7.5 billion with a group of 50 banks. The banks earned fees of about 2% of the loan commitments and interest rates about 1.74 percentage points over floating interest rates which is a strong incentive. The media merger specialists at CS First Boston who had been trying to line up financing for long-time client Ted Turner to acquire a television network may have been disappointed when he abruptly shifted gears; but whether Turner expanded by gobbling up a network or being taken over whole by a much bigger player like Time Warner the result added up to another multi-billion dollar deal to add to its long list of mergers and acquisitions.

Other winners in the multi-billion merger-madness were a smiling Laurence Tisch, CBS chairman who stood to make a profit of about US$970 million on the deal with Westinghouse; Ted Turner, as vice-chairman of Time Warner Inc., is to receive a five-year compensation package worth in excess of $100 million according to insiders familiar with the details; and, according to published reports, Michael Milken, banned for life from the securities industry and investment counselling, stands to make about $50 million for advising Turner on the sale of Turner Broadcasting to Time Warner.

If these are but a few of the winners there must be losers and these are likely to be consumers saddled with the costs of fat salaries, fat settlements and fat fees. The creative energies of the banking and financial systems appears to be concentrated far too heavily on monopoly games and financial gerrymandering rather than on the growth and development of the real economy. The shift in emphasis is a form of economic subversion.

THE GAMBLING BANKS

On June 16, 1994, at the invitation of the U.S. Consulate in Toronto, I had the privilege of attending a lunchtime seminar led by Howard Rosen, Executive Director of the U.S. Competitiveness Policy Council. Participants were shown slides indicating that U.S. competitiveness had suffered from inadequate investment in industry. The very low savings rate was cited as a matter of concern in this regard. When a slide was displayed which indicated the banks' collective investment in commercial real-estate, however, it appeared that the problem had not been as much a shortage of funds as it was the way the banks had been allocating resources – both the savings that had been entrusted to their stewardship and the new money they had been creating. Far too much had been allocated to Third World bonds, commercial real-estate and leveraged buyouts – which must be one of the most inflationary uses possible for bank-created money – leaving far too little for industrial expansion. U.S. competitiveness had been eroded because the tremendous power accruing to banks, including their licenses to create money, had not been used responsibly in the public interest.

Apart from the unfairness, the shift to very large, as opposed to small, business loans has been an economic disaster. When banks lent a few thousand dollars or a million or two to a small business for either start-up or expansion purposes, new jobs were created. But when they began to lend hundreds of millions or billions for takeovers, jobs were extinguished. When corporations were acquired at inflated prices it was inevitable that costs had to be cut in order to service the enormous debt. To become lean and mean was the buzzword. That meant firing people – often people who had worked for a company for years or decades. Using either the public's savings or newly-created money in this way has been a total perversion of economic theory and previous economic practice. Stripped of all the rhetoric, the banks have been financing higher costs (inflation) and job displacement (unemployment) at the same time.

The banks' real-estate loans became so irresponsible and attained such a high proportion of the total cost of development that the market went crazy. Values were inflated enormously and this contributed to the pressure to induce another recession. Governments were then left holding the bag. The banking system, led by the knights in shining armour at the Fed, began to contract the money supply and make life miserable for everyone. Interest rates rose, business slowed down, profits fell, government revenues declined and debts of governments soared.

INTERNATIONAL CONSEQUENCES

What banks do with their tremendous power to manufacture money obviously has international and global consequences of monumental proportions. Canadian banks, for instance, have often preferred to make loans to large American corporations wishing to buy up Canadian companies rather than to finance the development of Canada by Canadians.

They prefer the triple A guarantees of the foreign borrowers and have gone out of their way to wine and dine them.   Most takeovers of Canadian companies by foreigners, including Americans, were financed partially or wholly by Canadian banks.   The Canadian banks were quite willing to use the savings of Canadians and the near monopoly they have over the creation of money in a way which was detrimental to the public interest.   They were willing to sell an important part of Canadians' birthright in exchange for a few easy to manage loans.

Western banks, including both U.S. and Canadian banks, have been responsible for putting some of the poorest areas of the Third World into financial jeopardy.   They went through a phase when it was chic, because it seemed like an easy way to make money, to lend large sums to Third World governments with few guarantees as to how the money would be spent.   It may have been justice that some of the money wound up in Swiss banks and that the world's bankers were stuck with large write-downs of their highly questionable loans, but that isn't the end of the story.

Instead of the relatively rich Western world providing financial support as an "engine for development" to the struggling two-thirds of the planet, we have, for more than a decade, been a net financial drain on the "wretched of the earth".   As UNICEF shows in *The State of the World's Children, 1992, Summary*, our protectionism costs the Third World some $55 billion a year in lost exports, which is more than the total aid they receive.   Add the effects of protectionism to the weight of high cost loans and you have the international catastrophe that UNICEF reports.

"But it is, above all, the weight of past debts which threatens future progress ... the developing world owes approximately $1,300 billion to the governments and banks of the industrialized nations and to international financial institutions. Each year, the repayment of capital and interest amounts to approximately $150 billion – roughly three times as much as the developing world receives in aid.   As it is impossible to meet these interest charges in full, the amount unpaid is added to the total debt owed ...   When all transactions are taken into account – the net effect is that the developing world is now transferring $40 to $50 billion a year to the industrialized world."[9]

As the report indicates the emancipation of Africa is at stake. ... "Debt is the new slavery that has shackled the African continent. Sub-Saharan Africa owes approximately $150 billion. Each year, it struggles to pay about one third of the interest which falls due; the rest is simply added to the rising mountain of debt under which the hopes of the sub-continent lie buried. The total inhumanity of what is now appearing is reflected in the single fact that even the small proportion of the interest which Africa does manage to pay is absorbing a quarter of all its export earnings and costing the continent, each year, more than its total spending on the health and education of its people. Ten years of prevarication over this problem has already damaged not only the Africa of today but the Africa of tomorrow. While more than $10 billion a year in interest repayments in being sluiced out of that desperately poor continent, tens of millions of children are losing their one opportunity to grow normally, to go to school and become literate, and to acquire the skills necessary for their own and their countries' development in the years to come."[10] From a Western economic stability perspective one must ask how realistically such loans are treated on diverse balance sheets.

You might think that following their experience with questionable loans to real-estate developers, Third World governments and big highly-leveraged takeover schemes that banks would seek safe haven in a cycle of caution and conservatism. But that is not the case. Their penchant for gambling would appear to be congenital.

MORE BANK GAMBLING

Investing in bonds, for example, is considered to be conservative. If it is your own money, and there are unlikely to be circumstances requiring immediate liquidation, you can absorb a 10-20% loss in book value and just sit on the investment until it matures or until market conditions improve. Buying on margin, however, can put anyone at risk.

In the Spring of 1994 the bond market rout stunned many investors including some of the most savvy players. Long-term investors planning to hold bonds to maturity were not overly concerned. A number of traders, however, were badly hurt. The biggest losers were big New York firms such as Goldman, Sachs & Co., Bankers Trust New York Corp. and hedge-fund operators such as Michael Steinhardt and Julian Robertson.

Gambling on the price of bonds can be a costly business when you guess wrong. The case which is destined to be included in future economics textbooks is that of Toshihide Iguchi, an executive vice president in the New York operations of the Japanese Daiwa Bank, one of Japan's largest commercial banks. Iguchi managed to lose $1.1 billion over the last 11 years without detection by American or Japanese regulators. Officials on both sides of the ocean are scrambling around in an effort to determine how the deception was possible. Meanwhile it appears to be another classic lesson in the perils of letting one person both trade and keep books.

Another area in which banks gamble is foreign exchange. Not only do they put vast sums at risk, they build up a vested interest in monetary and exchange policies which may or may not be in their home country's interest. Holding sufficient reserves of foreign currencies to service their customers is both acceptable and desirable. When they start betting on currency markets, however, they add one more wild card to the banking game.

Of all the recent trends in banking the most alarming is the purchase and sale of derivatives. Just to read a brief lexicon of some of the different kinds of derivatives is enough to give one a bad headache. They include interest futures, interest options, currency futures, currency options, stock market index futures, options on stock market indices, interest rate swaps, currency and cross-currency interest rate swaps, just for starters. Some are so complicated that bank regulators themselves have a problem understanding them.

In the case of derivatives, too, there is a line between legitimate functions, such as hedging exchange rates for example, and pure gambling. Unfortunately the legitimate areas of swaps and options, designed to give buyers financial protection against adverse moves in such things as interest rates or foreign currencies, carry scant profits for the banks and securities firms that sell them. The big profits can only be realized from the exotic instruments but it takes a certain amount of expertise to craft them, so not every financial firm can compete. Those which have the capability find it a strong profit centre. For example, the profit for the seller on a typical leveraged swap runs about eight times the level of a traditional interest-rate swap. The more complex and customized the product becomes, the higher the fees the bank can command. So every bank of any size wants to sell exotic derivatives to its corporate customers.

Derivatives in general and exotic derivatives in particular constitute two extremely worrisome trends. The first is a further estrangement between the paper and real economies. Instead of concentrating on the growth of the real economy, banks concentrate their ingenuity and energy in playing the paper game. To encourage non-bankers to gamble, rather than promoting their core businesses, only compounds the felony.

Equally alarming, the banks have not been willing, until very recently, to disclose the extent of their exposure. The numbers are astronomical. "To those who assume the worst", reports *The Banker*, in its February 1993 issue, "the banks' deep involvement in the $10 trillion derivatives markets 'is an accident waiting to happen'. Few industries have done more than banking in recent years to validate Murphy's First Law: anything that can go wrong, will go wrong. Could derivatives, one of the most rapidly expanding and complex areas of financial activity, prove Murphy right, yet again?"[11]

If you ask the people who are making money from this form of gambling, there is nothing to worry about. If you ask the regulators who might lose their jobs if anything does go wrong, you get reactions varying from nonchalance to near apoplexy. In Canada a former Superintendent of Financial Institutions, Michael Mackenzie, issued guidelines to the banks but balked at the idea of imposing regulations. At the same time he admitted that were a major Canadian or U.S. financial institution to fail as the result of a derivatives book there could be a whole new ball game.

Holy mackerel! That is tantamount to the Federal Aeronautics Administration saying we have looked at the new high-flying saucer, we think it will fly all right because the manufacturers and test-pilots say so; but if one should crash, and a lot of innocent people are hurt, we will certainly take a closer look.

Well, a number of people have been hurt – such giants as Proctor & Gamble Co. of Cincinnati; Orange County, California, bankrupt thanks to gambling with derivatives and speculating on bonds with borrowed money. It's a long list topped by the Barings Bank of London, England which collapsed when 28 year-old Nick Leeson, in charge of a Barings outpost called Barings Futures (Singapore), committed the bank to ruinous speculations on the direction of Tokyo's Nikkei 225 stock index among other things.

Apologists for an unregulated industry argue that none of these disasters needed to happen. True, but they did. And the probability is that similar or worse will happen in the future. A 1995 study by Ernst & Young reported that despite last year's devastating losses from trading derivatives, many investment management companies still lack the ability to measure and control the risks associated with these exotic instruments.

Seventy-five percent of the companies studied don't employ risk-management teams independent of the company's trading function. Fifty-five percent permit traders to authorize the use of derivatives on the company's behalf. Nearly two-thirds don't use independent third parties to evaluate the logic behind pricing models used for over-the-counter, or non-exchange-traded derivatives.

This lack of supervision and control is the spawning ground for disaster. It only takes one rogue trader to do it. No bank is big enough to withstand a well-aimed "Singapore sling" and if it happened to be one of the big New York banks the domino effect could deflate the whole system which is far too-highly leveraged to withstand that kind of shock.

SUMMARY

From the end of the Korean War until the 1970s when anyone asked me if we could have another meltdown comparable to the early 1930s I said: "Impossible, we have learned so much from World War II and post-war experience, including demand management, that we will never allow anything that stupid again." I was wrong. The way things are going, anything could happen.

I find myself in complete agreement with economic journalist Robert J. Samuelson who ends his account of the Great Depression in the *Encyclopedia of Economics* this way. "Now it seems preventable. Then, it was baffling. World War I made restoration of the prewar economic system difficult, maybe impossible. But that is what world leaders attempted because it was all they knew and it had worked. Only its collapse convinced them to try something different. Old ideas were overtaken and overwhelmed. It has happened before – and could again."[12]

Indeed it could and most certainly will unless the banks are required to limit their gambling, increase their reserves, and change their priorities in order to bring the paper and real economies together in some sort of harmony.

CHAPTER 7

AN INFINITELY SILLY SYSTEM

"Taxation without representation is tyranny. "

James Otis

Can you imagine any congressman introducing a motion to this effect: "Be it resolved that the Congress of the United States hereby issues exclusive licences to chartered banks to manufacture all or nearly all of the new money put into circulation each year and to direct and divide it in accordance with their own best interests and those of their friends and close associates." Doesn't that strike you as silly? Yet that, in reality, is exactly what the Banking Act of 1935 did. It gave privately-owned chartered banks, regulated only by a federal reserve system owned by some of them, an exclusive mandate to manufacture or create money – apart from the small amount of treasury notes still in existence. Monetary sovereignty for the United States of America has been delegated to private banks.

The system is so silly that I really have difficulty knowing how to describe it. Normally I don't have too much difficulty coming up with appropriate adjectives. I've written six books, innumerable speeches and bi-weekly columns for ten years for the *Toronto Sun* and its syndicate *Canada Wide Features*. So I have had considerable practice in digging for words but in this case, I found, nothing seemed adequate. Ridiculous, inane, insane, grotesque, absurd and other adjectives crossed my mind but in each case they failed to portray the enormity of the situation and the outrage that fills my mind when I think how perverse the system really is. Finally, one evening, as I was contemplating the stars and distant galaxies, the word infinite came to mind. That was it. Our present monetary system is an infinitely silly system.

Some things are ironic in the extreme – indeed quite incomprehensible. Why would the people of the United States fight a war to gain independence from England because, in part, the mother country wouldn't permit the colonies to print their own currency while insisting that they borrow from British banks instead,[1] win the war and subsequently adopt the monetary scam practiced by the British goldsmiths? Especially when they had ingeniously experimented with an infinitely superior system.[2]

The fact that the British system, like measles, spread across the industrial world is one of the greatest tragedies of the two centuries since the industrial revolution began. Its spotty record of recurrent booms and busts has created untold heartache. Little wonder that there was an insistent cry for the establishment of central banks to regulate the excesses of the highly-leveraged, panic-prone, privately-owned banks. In the United States the Federal Reserve System was established in 1913, no doubt with high expectations. That these expectations have not been met is readily apparent to anyone who will take the time to read the record. Even some of the Fed's sponsors were soon disillusioned.

William Jennings Bryan, who acted as Democrat whip and is credited with a major effort in getting the Federal Reserve Act of 1913 passed, later said: "In my long political career, the one thing I genuinely regret is my part in getting the banking and currency legislation (FR Act) enacted into law."[3] Senator Carter Glass, one of the original sponsors of the Act of 1913, said on June 17, 1938: "I never thought the Federal

Bank System would prove such a failure. The country is in a state of irretrievable bankruptcy."[4] An early view from the Oval Office sounds the same note. President Woodrow Wilson, just 3 years after passage of the Act wrote: "A great industrial nation is controlled by its system of credit. Our system of credit is concentrated (in the Federal Reserve System). The growth of the nation, therefore, and all our activities are in the hands of a few men.... We have come to be one of the worst ruled, one of the most completely controlled and dominated governments in the civilized world."[5]

For "light" reading on a holiday in March, 1994, I took along *A Monetary History of the United States 1867-1960*, the 800 plus page opus by Milton Friedman and Anna Jacobson Schwartz. Reading it is enough to make one cry – or to get very, very angry, depending on the mood of the moment. It chronicles the failure of the system to provide consistent and measured monetary growth proportionate to the potential for increased goods and services; the inability of the Fed to prevent widescale bank failures; and the near-total paralysis of the system when it came to addressing the needs of the real economy, especially during the Great Depression.

THE GREAT DEPRESSION

As someone who had long believed that the Great Depression was the ultimate in economic folly I have been fascinated to learn that the term depression was applied to create the impression that the disaster which began in 1929 was in some way less severe than "panic", the word previously associated in the public's mind with severe economic downturns.[6] In retrospect it was just another ruse to mitigate the potential backlash from one more overdose of human misery when the banking system failed.

After the second banking crisis, in March, 1931, deepened the severity of the depression, President Hoover organized a nation-wide drive to assist private relief agencies in the Fall of that year. His committee of seventy was named the President's Unemployment Relief Organization. "The unemployed in many states formed self-help and barter organizations, with their own systems of scrip."[7] When the monetary system broke down the people, once again, as they had in earlier colonial days, invented their own money as a matter of necessity.

Will Rogers, the great American humorist and folk hero reported general agreement as to who was responsible for the monetary mess. On February 24, 1932, he warned that: "you can't get a room in Washington ... Every hotel is jammed to the doors with bankers from all over America to get their 'hand out' from the Reconstruction Finance Corporation ... And I have asked the following prominent men in America this question, 'What group have been more responsible for this financial mess, the farmers? ... Labor? ... Manufacturers? ... Tradesmen, or Who?' ... And every man – Henry Ford, Garner, Newt Baker, Borah, Curtis, and a real financier, Barney Baruch – without a moment's hesitation said, 'Why, the big bankers.' ... *Yet they have the honor of being the first group to go on the 'dole' in America!*"[8]

There may have been consensus as to who was responsible for the crisis but there was certainly no agreement on what to do about it. The contrasting attitudes of politicians, elected to serve the people, and the economic elite strikes a familiar chord.

"In Congress, however, there was growing support for increased government expenditures and for monetary expansion, proposals widely castigated by the business and financial community as 'greenbackism' and 'inflationary'. On its part, the business and financial community, and many outside it, regarded federal deficits as a major source of difficulty. Pressure to balance the budget finally resulted in the enactment of a substantial tax rise in June 1932. The strength of that sentiment, which, in light of present-day views seems hard to credit, is demonstrated by the fact that in the Presidential campaign of 1932, both candidates ran on platforms of financial orthodoxy, promising to balance the federal budget."[9] Doesn't that sound like déjà vu?

When the Federal Reserve Banks closed their doors on March 4, 1933, "The central banking system, set up primarily to render impossible the restriction of payments by commercial banks, itself joined the commercial banks in a more widespread, complete, and economically disturbing restriction of payments than had ever been experienced in the history of the country. One can certainly sympathize with Hoover's comment about that episode: 'I concluded [the Reserve Board] was indeed a weak reed for a nation to lean on in time of trouble.'"[10] Not only has there been little change in attitude since the 1930s, it appears that little has been learned from the experience. Americans still put their trust in a system regulated by a Fed which gives the interests of the banks and the money-lenders a higher priority than the interests of the country.

To the North, the Bank of Canada wasn't established until 1935. Prior to its establishment there appears to have been the usual difference of opinion between the bankers and ordinary people as to what its role should be. This dichotomy was summed up in an article in *Maclean's Magazine* in the summer of 1933.

"The point which our bankers seem to miss is that what the Canadian people want in a central bank is not to supply the other banks with rediscount facilities which they already have or to save us from future panics, [as, it is previously noted, U.S. experience shows they do not] but they do want an institution that will effectually control the whole of the money and credit of the nation, now under the control of the other banks, and which will somehow be able to make that money and credit available in sufficient volume wherever legitimately needed, and on terms much more fair and equitable than at present."[11] It was a pious hope that has not yet been realized.

To give them a little credit the Fed, in the U.S., and the Bank of Canada, in Canada, did help facilitate the financial requirements of World War II. They did this in two ways. First, they kept interest rates very low by buying and offering to buy government securities in the open market. Second, they increased their portfolios of government securities quite dramatically which was the equivalent of creating money for the government interest free, or virtually interest free. The interest paid to central banks on these securities was returned to government as profit so the net cost was close to zero. This kind of interest-free accommodation by central banks should not be confused with government-created debt-free money like Lincoln's greenbacks. One is included in the total debt that has to be repaid and the other is not.

U.S. High-Powered Money as a Percent of M3 (1946-1994)

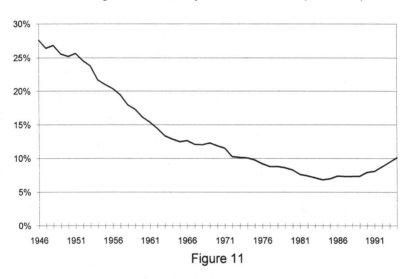

Figure 11

Source: IMF *Financial Statistics Yearbook*, 1970 and 1995

Even though the central banks were cooperative and provided government with more interest-free money in wartime than they had before, or have since, (Figure 11 shows the dramatic reduction in the proportion of interest-free money from 1946 until the mid-1980s) they stubbornly maintained the myth that it is privately-owned banking corporations which are endowed with the primary responsibility to "print" money. In the process government bonds were allowed as reserves for the banks in both countries so that the money lent to government became the basis on which the banks could create even more money with which to buy more government bonds.

It was the two decades after the war, including the fifteen golden years from roughly 1950-1965, when the system seemed to have found its stride. Growth was solid, jobs were available for people who wanted to work, inflation was modest, demand management was accepted as a legitimate concept and everyone seemed reasonably content with the economics profession. The ratio of total public and private debt to GDP in the United States fell from slightly above 165%, in 1946, to a low of 134%, in 1951, and then remained more or less constant in the 135-145% range for 30 years until 1981. It was only when the Fed adopted the monetarist "theology", and its consequent high interest rates, that the ratio began to rise again to a level of approximately 200% of GDP which is well above the 1946 peak.

THE 1981-82 AND 1990-91 RECESSIONS MADE A SILLY SYSTEM EVEN SILLIER

When Paul Volcker invoked "practical monetarism" he had reassuring words for Congress. "More positively stated, the progress we are clearly beginning to see on the inflation front when carried forward will help lay the base for recovery and much better economic performance over a long period of time."[12] While this was balm to the "true believers" it turned out to be a hollow promise. Not only has economic performance been worse, rather than better, floating interest rates have played havoc with the debt, both public and private.

Even, Milton Friedman, the Guru of monetarism, appears to be at sea when addressing the question of coping with the public debt. Following an address to the Fraser Institute in Vancouver, British Columbia, in May 1994, he was asked the following:

Question: "What shall we do with the problem of public debt which is beginning to swamp us all?"

Answer: "Well there's only one thing to do with it. There are only two ways you can handle the problem of public debt. You can either inflate it away or you can cut government spending, generate a surplus, or not even generate a surplus, just cut government spending. That will enable the economy to grow more rapidly and that will mean that the same government debt will become a smaller and smaller percentage of the income as you get a higher income. Those are the only two ways. There are no other ways to handle the public debt. You can't handle it by wishing it off and so you are either going to pay it off, you are either going to grow the economy in such a way that it becomes a bearable burden or else you're going to inflate it away. Those are the only things that can happen."[13]

Total Debt of Non-Financial Sectors (1976-1993)

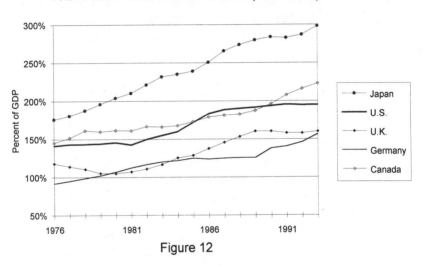

Figure 12

Source: IMF *Financial Statistics Yearbook* ; *Frankfurter Allgemeine Zeitung* , Sept. 7, 1995; Bank of Japan, *Flow of Funds* ; *The Building Society Industry in Transition* , L. Drake, 1989

Of course Prof. Friedman was asked specifically about the public debt and he acknowledged that it can't be paid off. Just to keep it from growing as a proportion of GDP is a monumental task. Had the question referred to total public and private debt, rather than just public debt, the answer is ten times more difficult. Under our present silly system of creating nearly all new money as debt there is neither any way to pay it off nor any practical way to prevent it from growing as a percentage of income to the point where the system will collapse of its own debt weight.

DEBTIZING THE MONEY

Haven't you ever wondered why just about any country you can think of is drowning in a sea of debt? As Figure 12 indicates, the total government and non-financial private debt of the United Kingdom and Germany is a little more than 150 percent of GDP, the United States approximately 200 percent, Canada about 225 percent and Japan about 300 percent. Do you really think that the entire burden of responsibility can be laid at the feet of profligate politicians? I have known a few thousand politicians in the course of my career and it is my opinion, based on careful observation, that they are just as dedicated, just as well educated, just as sincere, just as well motivated, and just as honest as the people who elect them. If that isn't good enough, then the problem is more general. In fact they take too much of their advice from the wrong people and much of it is bad advice. I would include in that select group central bankers, bankers, financiers, financial writers and most economists.

The reason that all industrial societies are so far in debt is that most of their money is created by privately-owned banks as debt. Period! The interest on those bank loans is additional debt – additional debt which is usually paid (if that is an appropriate term) by further borrowing. To the extent that growth of the real economy is dependent on a fresh infusion of new money each year that infusion will only occur if someone is willing to go further into debt in the process. If people are either unable or unwilling to borrow, as in the 1930s, the economy will stagnate.

GOVERNMENT DEFICITS

How many times have you read that government deficits were responsible for most of our economic ills. When they're not being blamed for inflation, a responsibility that was usually over-stated except in wartime or national emergency, they're blamed for high interest rates. Government borrowing, it is alleged, competes with private borrowing and thus drives up the cost of money in the marketplace.

There is another, more positive, function which is seldom mentioned. An economy expands in response to business investment, consumer demand, export demand and government spending. When the first three of these are insufficient to keep the economy growing at its potential, additional government spending is required to take up the slack. This fact is not admitted by conservative economists who insist that all governments must do is establish a climate of confidence. Then business will expand and provide the necessary jobs. Alas, that is not the experience of the last 200 years.

In 1932, for example, a demand to reduce the deficit and balance the federal budget led to a general tax increase. But every dollar taken out of the economy in tax revenue is one less dollar that individuals and companies have left to spend or invest. When the money they have left is inadequate to keep the economy growing at its potential, it doesn't grow at its potential. It is a sad commentary on mainline economists that it took about 150 years after the industrial revolution before they were willing to admit that fact. They took refuge in Say's law which states that all production creates an equal and opposite demand – one more fine theory which didn't pass muster in the real world. It was only when John Maynard Keynes underscored the obvious that his fellow economists took note.

I have seldom known a business that wouldn't bend heaven and earth to find the capital or credit necessary to expand in order to meet a demand for the goods and services it produces and it matters little whether the demand is consumer-driven or government-driven. When consumer demand is slack, and the average person is unable or unwilling to borrow more and go deeper into debt, it has often been government, which has a great capacity to borrow, that has been willing to assume more debt in order to stimulate the economy and get it moving.

Never has this been more true than it was to end the Great Depression and gear up the economy to wage World War II. It was government expenditures which provided the jobs and stimulated the previously moribund economy until it was working to capacity. In that case it was a combination of bank-created money (credit) and Fed-created interest-free money that made it possible to end the depression, finance the war and lay the foundation for the best twenty-five years that Western capitalism has ever known.

MONETIZING THE DEBT

In the course of a guest lecture at the University of Windsor in September, 1995, I was asked if, by printing money, a government was not just monetizing the debt. An observer told me later that as soon as the subject was raised peoples' eyes just glazed over. I can understand why, really, because the subject is not your number one science thriller. Still it is an important subject and not too difficult once you have a grasp of what money is and where it comes from.

When Secretary of the Treasury Hugh McCulloch, in 1865, exchanged government bonds for previously issued Lincoln greenbacks he was debtizing the money. People were given interest-bearing bonds in exchange for non-interest-bearing greenbacks (cash). When banks create money by making loans they create money (credit) and debt (notes payable) simultaneously. When banks create money to buy government bonds they credit "money" to the government's account in exchange for bonds. The government spends the money (credit) to pay its bills but it still owes the bank for the principal amount of the bonds and any interest due in respect of them. When the Fed prints cash to buy government bonds from the banking system it is in fact monetizing that much of the debt.

In Western capitalist economies, with their fractional reserve banking systems, i.e. where banks have very little cash to back up their deposits and, instead, hold most of their assets in bonds, stocks, loans, mortgages, and other interest-bearing investments, the whole system rests on faith in credit's ultimate convertibility into money. In the U.S. it is the faith that the Fed would run the printing presses day and night in the event there was a serious run on the nation's banks, i.e. that the Fed would monetize enough debt to provide the banks with liquidity and satisfy the demands of depositors.

That is the one area in which the Fed appears to have learned a little since the Great Depression. A careful reading of *The Confidence Game*, by Steven Solomon, shows that the Fed has charged to the rescue of the banking system time and again. In fact, today, the Fed appears to be little more than a mother hen for the private banks. It is quite willing to protect their interests at the taxpayers expense.

What the Fed has not learned is how to control the economy in the best interests of taxpayers at large. The same can be said for most other central banks. Under the circumstances, one of the worst ideas being promulgated in the world today is that central banks should be independent of both governments and congresses or parliaments. They should not! To give them total independence would be a complete abrogation of government of, by and for the people. It would be a return to slavery – the slavery of slow growth and intolerable debt.

THE ROLE OF CENTRAL BANKS

Any country with a monetary system based primarily on credit has to have a central bank available to monetize debt in case of emergency. The bankers have a more polite way of saying it. They say that a principal role of any central bank is to act as "lender of last resort". But if you translate that into understandable English it means that a principal role of any central bank is to print cash money and trade it for government bonds or other securities when the banks' customers decide they want to hold their money in cash. The process of printing cash with which to buy government bonds is, purely and simply, converting debt into money which is monetizing debt.

Of course central banks have the additional function of regulating the total amount of money in the system (cash and credit) and of influencing the price of money (interest rates) by increasing or decreasing the supply. This is raw power.

It is the kind of raw power which allows central banks to make or break governments by frustrating their policies.

It should be obvious from glancing at the data that any reprise of the post-World War II improvement in the ratio of federal debt to GDP will require strong growth and low interest rates, i.e. federal borrowing rates no greater than the growth rate of GDP if the existing debt is to be accommodated without further increases in taxes. So what did the Fed, led by Chairman Alan Greenspan do? After just a few weeks of robust growth in 1994 the screws were turned, interest rates increased, and the rate of growth slowed when there was still some slack in the economy and involuntary unemployment, which is not "natural", remained at a morally unacceptable rate for a civilized country.

Not only that, the Fed's 1994 increases in interest rates played havoc with markets both in the U.S. and elsewhere. Stocks and bonds plummeted. In Canada, where there had not yet been anything like robust growth, interest rates rose to put a further damper on a recovery that could only be described as fragile, at best. The question arises as to whether central bankers in their blind pursuit of price stability really have any idea what they are doing to real economies and real governments? Does it make sense to raise interest rates, increase the cost of servicing government debt, and put additional strain on deficits?

First the central bankers, with the private banks cheering them on, induced the recessions that put governments deeper and deeper in debt and made it almost impossible for them to balance their budgets. Then senior bank officials started making speeches about how the country should be run. Governments should raise taxes, but not in the area of financial transactions where there is a lot of loose change to be found. They should cut programs. They shouldn't spend more money on infrastructure, housing or health care because, if they do, markets will add a premium to the rate they charge on the money they lend to them.

It is my strong conviction that private banks should not have been given the power to manufacture money to lend to federal governments at interest. This is a gift which the banks did nothing to earn. Worse, it is a form of taxation. When banks lend newly-created money to governments (the people) they are guaranteed that the government will tax the people in order to repay both principal and interest. Isn't that unconstitutional? You even have private banks in other countries creating money to convert into U.S. currency for the purpose of buying U.S. government bonds. Is there no limit to the scam?

When you survey the damage wrought by central bankers, who act as if they are accountable to no one, you wonder about the "leaders", especially economists, who want to entrench that despotic power. The most powerful economic weapon in the entire arsenal is to be entrusted to someone at arms length from responsibility? Marriner Eccles may have been a "smart cookie", as one of my friends describes him, but only a banker would have advised Franklin D. Roosevelt to establish a seven-man Federal Reserve Board at arms length to the Treasury.

In Canada and the United Kingdom governments have retained ultimate responsibility in theory, at least, if not in practice. But there are advocates of completely independent central banks modelled on the Bundesbank. If I were someone living in the European community I would live in fear and dread of a single currency in the hands of bankers trained in that school. The interests of the usurers would take preference over all other human interests. The paper economy would prevail.

The worst and most frightening of competing ideas on monetary reform comes from Harvard economist and former Under Secretary for Economic Affairs, Richard N. Cooper. In a paper entitled "A Monetary System for the Future" he proposes the creation of a common currency for all the major western industrialized countries with a common monetary policy and a joint Bank of Issue.[14] The Bank of Issue, with overall responsibility for determining monetary policy, would be governed by a board made up of representatives of national governments whose votes would be weighted according to the share of their country's gross national product to the total GNP of the community of participating nations.

A principal purpose of the proposed "reform" would be to reduce the fluctuations in real exchange rates which is another way of saying that the interests of citizens of individual countries must be subordinate, in the future, as they often have been in the past, to the interests of international finance. National governments might exercise some influence with their own nominee, in theory, but in fact they would no longer be able to pursue any kind of independent monetary policy. Sovereignty over the most powerful of all economic tools would be turned over to an international monetary monster.

A world bank run by a world kingship of international appointees collectively not accountable to anyone? Heavenly days! Has the man of letters never heard of the Magna Carta? And what about the American War for Independence to free these United States from taxation without representation?

Allons enfants de la patrie, le jour de gloire est arrivé. Where are the farmers with their pitchforks? Where are the workers with their baseball bats and shotguns? It's time for another revolution! But this time a revolution of the mind!

CHAPTER 8

RE-INVENTING THE WHEEL

"All great truths begin as blasphemies."

George Bernard Shaw

I was somewhat astonished to learn a couple of years ago that Nobel laureate Milton Friedman has long been an advocate of monetary reform. He had been associated in my mind with two theories, monetarism and a "natural rate" of unemployment, which, in their application to the real economy, I consider to be the two most unfortunate ideas to come on the economic stage since the Great Depression. It was with surprise and pleasure, then, that I found his name amongst the handful of pioneers who advocate an end to the fractional reserve system of banking and the substitution of a 100 percent reserve system.

First in an article entitled "A Monetary and Fiscal Framework for Economic Stability" published in the *American Economic Review*, in 1948,[1] and later in *A Program for Monetary Stability*, published in 1959,[2] Friedman makes the case for fundamental change. In the book he wrote: "As a student of Henry Simons and Lloyd Mints, I am naturally inclined to take the fractional reserve character of our commercial

100

banking system as the focal point in a discussion of banking reform. I shall follow them also in recommending that the present system be replaced by one in which 100% reserves are required."[3]

I was even more surprised to learn that the economist whose work had influenced me the most at university, Irving Fisher, had also recommended a 100% reserve system of banking. It was his theory of money which first convinced me that recessions and depressions were monetary phenomena and, by extension, totally unnecessary. Not until the winter of 1993, however, did I become aware of his *100% Money*[4] and took the opportunity to read it. A man whose advice, had it been taken, would have helped us escape the worst ravages of the Great Depression, Fisher deserves a place high on the list of the great economists of all time.

Of course the idea of substituting government-created money for bank-created money was not original with these men despite the A+ they deserve for recognizing the merit of the concept. As we saw in Chapter 5, the American colonies had conducted experiments with government-created money as an alternative to borrowing from British banks. In Pennsylvania, for example, within a few years after it began to put paper money into circulation, with mortgaged real-estate as security, a remarkable revival of its economy took place. It was reported that in Philadelphia in 1726, twice the number of ships were built as in any year previously.[5]

LINCOLN AND GOVERNMENT-CREATED MONEY

Although Abraham Lincoln was not a proponent of government-created money, he certainly recognized its usefulness in time of emergency. In his December 1862 message to Congress, Lincoln made the following reference to greenbacks: "The suspension of specie payments by banks soon after the commencement of your last session, made large issues of United States Notes [greenbacks] unavoidable. In no other way could the payment of the troops, and the satisfaction of other just demands, be so economically or so well provided for. The judicious legislation of Congress, securing the receivability of these notes for loans and internal duties, and making them a legal tender for other debts, has made them a universal currency; and has satisfied, partially, at least, and for the time, the long-felt want of an uniform circulating medium, saving thereby to the people immense sums in discounts and exchanges."[6]

There was some Congressional support for adopting the system on a permanent basis. Representative Thaddeus Stevens, first elected to Congress as a Whig and later as a Republican, in speaking during the spirited debates over the first of the Legal Tender Acts, prior to the enactment of the legislation authorizing the printing of greenbacks,[7] said: "The government and not the banks should have the profit from creating a medium of exchange."[8] Another booster was Alexander Campbell, a mining engineer and entrepreneur, elected to Congress from Illinois in 1874 for a single term on a Democrat-Independent ticket. In *The True Greenback* he wrote: "The war has resulted in the complete overthrow and utter extinction of chattle slavery on this continent, but it has not destroyed the principle of oppression and wrong. The old pro-slaver serpent, beaten in the South, crawled up North and put on anti-slavery clothes and established his headquarters in Wall Street where ... he now, through bank monopolies and non-taxed bonds, rules the nation more despotically than under the old regime. ... I assert ... that an investment of a million dollars under the National Banking Law, or in non-taxed government securities, will yield a larger net income to its owner than a like amount invested in land and slaves employed in raising cotton and sugar did in the South in the palmiest days of the oligarchy."[9]

It was the bankers' view which carried the day, however. In March, 1865, President Lincoln appointed a banker, Hugh McCulloch, secretary of the treasury. In a speech at Ft. Wayne, Indiana, in 1868, McCulloch said: "I look upon an irredeemable paper currency as an evil.... Gold and silver are the only true measures of value. I have myself no more doubt that these metals were prepared by the Almighty for this very purpose."[10]

Of course McCulloch's view of the Almighty did not end the controversy. Farmers, in particular, kept it alive. As grain prices fluctuated precariously, they became increasingly infuriated at what they considered to be usurious interest rates demanded by the banks, and government largesse toward the railroads. "The government had given four western railroads as much land as Ohio, Indiana, Michigan, and Wisconsin together, in addition to millions of dollars in loans or outright subsidies."[11] The farmers' acute unhappiness led to a kind of populism which embraced both the nationalization of money-creation and of the railroads. The platform of the People's Party of America in 1892, for example, called for "a national currency, safe, sound, and flexible, issued by the General Government only, a full legal tender for all debts, public and private, and this without the use of banking corporations.... the government to own and operate the railroads in the interest of the people."[12] Their presidential candidate, Brigadier General James Baird Weaver, received more than a million votes in the 1892 election but the movement eventually petered out and the bankers' orthodoxy prevailed.

CANADA AND SOCIAL CREDIT

Canadian opinion, as is often the case, parallelled that south of the border. Western farmers nursed the same two pet hates – the banks and the railroads. The boiling point came during the Great Depression when western unrest spawned new populist political parties including one called Social Credit, based primarily on the concept of monetary reform. It began as a provincial party which formed a government in Alberta, in 1935, where it tried to put its beliefs into practice. The Supreme Court of Canada ruled the attempt unconstitutional because money and banking were the exclusive responsibility of the federal government.

Undeterred, the Social Crediters formed a federal party and elected a strong block of MPs who were already in Ottawa when I became a neophyte member in 1949. Their leader was Solon E. Low, an articulate Albertan backed by others including

Victor Quelch, MP for Acadia, and probably the most respected of the theorists, and John Blackmore, a Mormon priest who hammered away at the subject so consistently that there was a time when I could have repeated his remarks almost verbatim from memory.

Solon Low spoke for his party in criticizing the existing system. "Let us for a moment take a look at the financial and money system of these fellows who run the government", he said. "They believe that before we can add to the national wealth we must go out to the money brokers and borrow enough to complete or develop any one of our national resources and then pay interest to the money brokers for the use of our own money. We Canadians, therefore, are compelled to add to the national debt every time we wish to add to the national wealth. They call that sensible – the very people who ignorantly refer to social credit as funny money!"[13]

The substance of their concern can be summed up in two brief quotes. The first from John Blackmore, "What Social Crediters have advocated is to create enough money and to put it into circulation in the right places to enable the purchasing power of the people to equal the amount of goods on sale on the market."[14] The second, as expressed by a subsequent leader of the party, Robert Thompson, is the one that kept ringing in my ears: "Our aim is to make financially possible what is physically possible."[15] In effect Thompson was proposing a marriage of the physical and paper economies.

The Social Credit party, and its predecessor the Social Credit League, had been inspired, at least in part, by the writings of Major C.H. Douglas, a British engineer who, like a lot of ordinary people, gifted with a certain amount of common sense, had observed the periodic shortage of purchasing power in the British economy. To explain his position, Major Douglas employed his celebrated "A + B" theorem, in which he divided all costs of production into two categories. The "A" costs included all payments that producers (factories) made to individuals, such as wages, salaries and dividends, the "B" costs included all payments made to organizations for such things as raw materials, machinery, maintenance of plant, bank charges, etc. Thus for any period, the total costs of production were represented by A + B, but the amount of money available to purchase the output of the period was only A, because B costs were largely in the nature of business "reserves", mere bookkeeping items which, while included in total costs of production, did not represent income distributed.[16]

The theorem was an abstraction that didn't add up and consequently was ripped to shreds by the classical economists. Some of the things that Douglas identified, however, were perfectly valid. The periodic shortage of purchasing power, for example, would later be acknowledged by Keynes. In this respect both men questioned the validity of Say's law which had been such an impediment to the development of economic thought. Say's law was incorrect when it suggested that all production creates an equal and opposite demand. It obviously hadn't and to pretend otherwise was a stumbling block of monumental proportions. A fundamental difference in principle between Douglas and Keynes, who lumped the engineer in with Marx as "underworld figures",[17] was in their method of filling the purchasing gap. Douglas would use government-created money – too much as he proposed it – while Keynes would have governments borrow their way to prosperity in the belief that eventually equilibrium would be restored and the extra debt would be repaid.

The A + B theorem didn't make sense. But one could easily conclude that there were problems involved in trying to borrow your way to prosperity and that somehow the gap between the purchasing power available and the amount required to clear the market had to be filled. This was the missing link that my professors could never come up with at university. They knew the gap existed; they knew that there was a periodic shortage of purchasing power even if they couldn't or wouldn't explain why; but they had no suggestions when it came to a mechanism for closing the gap and equating demand with supply in the long run. It was a subject which you couldn't talk about because most people didn't understand it and those who had been trained in economics were too impatient to listen.

VOICES CRYING IN THE WILDERNESS

For two centuries the debate concerning monetary matters has ebbed and flowed. It was certainly a factor leading up to the War for Independence. Then, in the early days of the Republic, the subject was a question for passionate debate between Thomas Jefferson and Alexander Hamilton. The Jeffersonian view, which attracted a wide following, can be summed up in the following quote: "I believe, that banking institutions are more dangerous to our liberties than standing armies. The issuing power should be taken from the banks and restored to the people to whom it properly belongs." Notwithstanding Jefferson's strongly-worded plea on behalf of monetary sovereignty it was Hamilton's preference for the British banking system which ultimately prevailed.

The subject boiled to the surface again near the end of the nineteenth century when the populists succeeded in gaining widespread support. It seems that whenever the economy was in serious trouble a debate on monetary reform erupted like an old volcano only to be forgotten as the crisis cooled and better times prevailed. In this case it was the discovery of gold in California which provided the stimulus necessary to stifle dissent.

It was the Great Depression of the 1930s which renewed the intellectual ferment both in academic and political circles. In the face of a banking system in crisis, in 1933, a number of economists at the University of Chicago produced what later became known as the Chicago Plan. It called for outright public ownership of the Federal Reserve Banks and the establishment of new institutions that accepted only demand deposits subject to a 100 percent reserve requirement in lawful money and/or deposits with the Reserve's Banks.[18]

One of the eight signatories of the six-page memorandum outlining the plan was Professor H.C. Simons. Three years later, in March 1936, he summed up succinctly the essence of his concern. "Given release from a preposterous financial structure, capitalism might endure indefinitely its other afflictions; but, assuming continuance of our financial follies..., it becomes academic to consider how the system might be saved."[19]

A Canadian prime minister, William Lyon Mackenzie King shared the concerns being expressed south of the border. In 1935 he said: "Once a nation parts with control of its currency and credit, it matters not who makes that nation's laws. Usury, once in control, will wreck any nation. Until the control of currency and credit is restored to government and recognized as its most conspicuous and sacred responsibility, all talk of the sovereignty of Parliament and of democracy is idle and futile."[20]

Debate on the subject of monetary reform didn't end with World War II. As I indicated, the Social Credit Party made a valiant effort to keep it alive in the Canadian Parliament while knowledgeable congressmen like Wright Patman, long-time chairman of the House Committee on Banking and Currency, fought for significant changes in the U.S. system. Alas, their pleas fell on deaf ears because times were too good to generate public demand for change.

By the time Western economies again began to go awry a new breed of University of Chicago economists, far removed from their predecessors of the 1930s, developed a different plan called monetarism which they promoted vigorously. Their ideas swept across the industrialized world like an Arctic air mass in winter. The deep freeze was so severe that the intellectual juices stopped flowing. Except for isolated oases, the climate was too unforgiving for rational debate.

It was only when an impending debt crisis appeared on the horizon that interest in alternatives began to re-emerge. To date, there has been very little room for dissent in the face of the conventional "slash and burn" orthodoxy borrowed from the 1930s. But there are a few reform buds pushing through the winter sod. Tentative, still, but could they be a harbinger of spring?

DEBT-FREE MONEY RESURFACES

There have been few public proponents of the concept

of debt-free money for many years until recently when the idea resurfaced. One spokesman is a bright and very articulate young Canadian, Jordan Grant, president of Seaton Group and chairman of the Bank of Canada for Canadians Coalition. In a paper entitled "Reintegrating Monetary Policy Into the Economic Tool Kit" which he sent as an appendix to a February 4, 1994, letter to Gordon Thiessen, the new Governor of the Bank of Canada, one of Grant's proposals related to the $6 billion municipal infrastructure program which had been a key part of the platform of the new Liberal government elected in October, 1993. Grant's suggestion read as follows: "Given the severity of our current problems, we need to be pragmatic in looking for solutions. Under the existing legislation, the Bank of Canada can finance the entire $6-billion infrastructure program, provided the municipal debentures are guaranteed by either the federal or provincial levels. Let's do it as a first step. We can then assess its impact and determine whether or how far we should shift the balance of government borrowing and money creation from private lenders back towards the Bank of Canada. Increasing the proportion of effectively interest-free money and eliminating our reliance on foreign borrowing is the means to holding down the general level of interest rates. Such a shift is the key to reducing the government's single largest area of expenditure – interest on the public debt."[21]

THE SOVEREIGNTY PROPOSAL

A more comprehensive suggestion has been put forward in the United States by Kenneth Bohnsack. For several years he has been proposing that the United States Treasury be directed to create money and lend it, interest free, to junior tax supported bodies for voter-approved capital projects. It is called the "Sovereignty Proposal". Perhaps it isn't too surprising that the idea has been much more favorably received by the intended recipients than by those who would be charged with the implementation. I am advised that 1,828 tax supported bodies have endorsed the plan, as well as the U.S. Conference of Mayors representing 1,050 cities of 30,000 or more, where

80 million Americans reside; also the Bankers Association of Illinois, representing some 500 small banks, in addition to the House and Senate of Michigan.[22] Still the Sovereignty Proposal has many hurdles to overcome before the idea is accepted in mainstream economics.

In Canada a variant of the Bohnsack proposal was put forward by Jack Biddell in his 1993 book *A Self Reliant Future for Canada*. Biddell is one of Canada's best known and most respected accountants and trustees in bankruptcy. He has also had extensive experience in the administration of incomes policies and knows first-hand the consequences of the irrational monetary policy followed in recent years. His suggestion is the formation of two Bank of Canada funds bearing interest at 1 percent. Facility A would be a $100 billion debt refinancing fund which would allow the provincial governments to replace high interest debt with low as the existing debt matured. Facility B would be a $200 billion loan to the federal and provincial governments to be drawn on over the next 20 years. The B Facility would be divided into B1, a $175 billion pool for capital expenditures and/or industrial investment, and a B2 pool of $25 billion for deficit financing. The money for infrastructure would be repaid over the life of the bridge, tunnel or filtration plant being built.[23]

THE DEAD WEIGHT OF DOGMATISM

As I ponder the reasons why ideas which are so obviously beneficial to the public weal should be so deeply buried in the dust-covered book shelves of public libraries and public consciousness several come to mind. First, and most important, people don't understand the concept. And politicians, believe it or not, are people too and they don't understand it; so whenever they receive a submission on the subject they refer it to their congressional or parliamentary research staff for "expert" comment. The analyses are totally predictable. I have read a number of them and they are almost embarrassing in their "the sun does revolve 'round the earth and it's baloney to think otherwise" brand of dogmatism.

Occasionally I have known a politician who would understand and admit publicly to being intrigued by the potential. One, I remember, was a long-ago mayor of Vancouver, Gerald (Gerry) DeGeer.[24] But his monetary views were considered an aberration and tolerated by a skeptical press only because he was so popular on every other front.

I often listened to the Social Credit MPs debate and was interested in what they had to say, but remained silent. I sometimes wondered if anyone else on the government benches felt the same way. You can imagine my astonishment when one day, as I was standing behind the curtain of the House of Commons, where we often stood when we were only half listening or when those who smoked wished to have a cigarette, one of my senior colleagues, David Croll, said "You know, what they are saying makes a lot of sense." I was flabbergasted. David Croll was on the left wing of the Liberal party and the Social Crediters were perceived as being on the far right. Croll had served his country in wartime, been mayor of Windsor, a cabinet minister in the provincial government of Ontario and resigned his portfolio during the dispute between the United Automobile Workers and General Motors of Canada when the union was trying to get a toe-hold. Croll's immortal line was "I would rather walk with the UAW than ride with General Motors." So anyone who knew him, and what he stood for, would have been as surprised as I was to hear him admit that a fundamental reform of the monetary system made sense.

I was perfectly aware, however, that if a reporter had stopped him on the way out of the House and asked him what he thought of the Social Credit speech just delivered he would have mumbled something like "nonsense" and dashed off. It would be hypocritical of me to suggest that I would have done otherwise. I don't know what I would have said but it certainly wouldn't have been complimentary. If either of us had been forthright we would have been labeled "nut cakes" or something equally unflattering.

To put it bluntly, we were intimidated by the press. I doubt that there were more than two or three of the several hundred reporters in the parliamentary press gallery who had the vaguest notion of how money was created and how the monetary system operated; and they were the ones who were not widely read. Syndicated columnists like Southam News' Charlie Lynch, for example, would just bellow "funny money" and go into hysterics anytime the subject was even alluded to. I hate to think what Charlie would have written about any allegedly "respected" member of one the major parties who uttered a sympathetic word.

For all his skill at writing Lynch was not particularly analytical. When I think of him I'm reminded of a chance meeting with Rabbi Abraham Feinberg of Toronto's Holy Blossom Synagogue at what is now Pearson International Airport. After exchanging a few pleasantries he said: "You politicians are just like us clergymen; too much time spent travelling and talking and not enough spent reading and thinking." I don't think it would be too unkind to put Charlie, who died after this section was written, in the same boat with the politicians he wrote about. No doubt he was influenced by the many bank and securities firm economists who are routinely quoted by the media. It is assumed that they are neutral because they are economists but in fact they have a powerful vested interest in perpetuating the present system.

A second and related problem was that in Canada, at least, the Social Credit Party sometimes colored the objectivity of their case by alleging an international conspiracy of bankers. Conspiracy theories are never popular with mainstream politicians so that was reason enough for the majority to "tune out". Worse, there was occasionally just a whiff of anti-Semitism in the background. This was resented, and justly so. It was true that the Rothschilds had understood the advantages of fractional reserve banking and had used their knowledge skilfully to put scme European governments deeply in their debt.[25] But the same can be said for Italian, French, Canadian, American, German and Japanese bankers. The cupidity of the bankers is less the result of a conspiracy on their part than a by-product of limited understanding on the part of governments and their electors.

A third obstacle has been the exaggerated claims of some monetary enthusiasts. A tabloid that arrived in my mail in July, 1994, proclaimed in respect of the Bank of Canada creation of debt-free money: "This will mean the end of debts, taxes, unemployment, bankruptcies, crises, wars!"[26] The claim is so ridiculous that it must be dismissed as fantasy. Regrettably the grain of truth was drowned in a sea of hyperbole.

Another impediment has been a confusion of specifics. My files contain at least a dozen proposals of which no two are the same. In Irving Fisher's *100% Money*, for example, he proposed the establishment of a "Currency Commission" which would buy bank assets for cash to the point where every commercial bank would have a cash reserve equal to 100% of its checking deposits – a state it would be required to maintain. As the banks would lose a large part of their interest-bearing assets they would be required to recover the lost income through service charges to their depositors.[27] Little wonder, then, that although Fisher managed to find two prominent bankers willing to support the idea the majority were strongly opposed.

Milton Friedman, well aware of the necessity to neutralize the bankers' objections, proposed paying interest on the 100% reserves. In *A Program For Monetary Stability* he said the following. "I shall depart from the original 'Chicago Plan of Banking Reform' in only one respect, though one that I think is of great importance. I shall urge that interest be paid on the 100% reserves. This step will both improve the economic results yielded by the 100% reserve system, and also, as a necessary consequence, render the system less subject to the difficulties of avoidance that were the bug-a-boo of the earlier proposals."[28] One of the serious problems, however, was what the rate of interest should be. "This problem of how to set the rate of interest is another issue that I feel most uncertain about and that requires more attention than I have given to it."[29] This is a concern I share and especially when I know how difficult it would be to ensure objectivity when banks are such generous supporters of the political system.

Of the other proposals I have mentioned each is limited in scope. Jordan Grant's recommendation was limited to pump priming to see how a revised system would work. Kenneth

Bohnsack is proposing money creation for specific purposes in the realm of state and city infrastructure. Jack Biddell is proposing money for debt refinancing, infrastructure and deficit financing in Canada. In both the Bohnsack and Biddell proposals the funds would be earmarked for specific purposes and one wonders if that is necessarily the most efficient use of resources – especially if we are talking about long-term as opposed to short-term resolution of the monetary system.

In the next chapter I will propose a variation on the theme which is intended to be general as opposed to specific in its application, and long-term as opposed to short-term in horizon. It is designed to stand the test of time, at least for a generation, after which such adjustments can be made as are deemed expedient on the basis of experience.

CONCLUSION

The concept of government-created debt-free money is time-honored and solid. It has had the support of people as diverse in background as Thomas Jefferson, H.C. Simons, William Lyon Mackenzie King and Henry Ford – all men of intelligence. Their views were reinforced for me by numerous conversations with the late Graham Towers, the first Governor of the Bank of Canada and one of the best financial minds Canada has produced. He allayed any residual fears that I might have had. He compared government-created money to Coca Cola and said "a bottle or two could be very refreshing whereas drinking a whole case at one sitting might kill you." These were wise words from a wise man who, throughout his career, always lived and upheld the maxim "moderation in all things."

CHAPTER 9

A 50% SOLUTION

*"Throw no gyft agayne at the gevers head for better
is halfe a lofe than no bread."*

John Haywood

Monetary reform alone will not get us out of the super
mess in which we have got the economy. Other measures, to
be discussed in subsequent chapters, are required. A revolutionary change in the way money is created, however, is the
bedrock foundation on which a more stable and enduring system
can be built. Without monetary reform the whole economic
superstructure will sink deeper and deeper into debt.

Bank "admirers", with a penchant for vengeance, might
fantasize a solution along the lines of the one adopted by
England's King Charles II. He just repudiated liability for the
deposits held in the Exchequer.

"This King being always in want of money, and not
wishing to go before the House of Commons, took counsel of
his ministers as to the best way of obtaining money without the
aid of Parliament. The King promised a reward of the Lord
Treasurer's post to whoever would suggest the means. The idea
of closing the Exchequer occurred to Lord Ashley, who un-
guardedly communicated it to Sir Thomas Clifford, and he
immediately unfolded the plan before the King, who was

charmed at the idea of such perfidy, and exclaimed: 'Odds fish! I will be as good as my word if you can find me the money.' Accordingly the Exchequer was closed on the 2nd of January 1672, and all payments to the goldsmith-bankers suspended; this not only brought ruin to them, but to many thousands of their customers.   Sir Thomas Clifford was made Lord High Treasurer and a peer."[1]

It was only intended as a temporary measure and some interest was subsequently paid; but the goldsmiths never did get their money back.[2] It was an extreme solution and not really appropriate to Charles' time or ours.

Somewhat less extreme was Yale economist Irving Fisher's suggestion that the banks be required to exchange their interest-bearing assets for cash (to be provided by a 'Currency Commission' on behalf of the government) up to an amount equal to 100% of their checking deposits.[3] It is still interesting, decades later when the Great Depression is only a distant memory, to read the list of advantages Fisher said would accrue to the public. They are as follows:

"1. There would be practically no more runs on commercial banks; because 100% of the depositors' money would always be in the bank (or available) awaiting their orders. In practice, less money would be withdrawn than now; we all know of the frightened depositor who shouted to the bank teller 'If you haven't got my money, I want it; if you have, I don't'.

2. There would be far fewer bank failures; because the important creditors of a commercial bank who would be most likely to make it fail are its depositors, and these depositors would be 100% provided for.

3. The interest-bearing Government debt would be substantially reduced; because a great part of the outstanding bonds of the Government would be acquired from the banks by the Currency Commission (representing the Government).

4. Our monetary system would be simplified; because there would be no longer any essential difference between pocket-book money and check-book money. All of our circulating medium, one hundred per cent of it, would be actual money.

5. Banking would be simplified; at present, there is a confusion of ownership. When money is deposited in a checking account, the depositor still thinks of that money as his, though legally it is the bank's. The depositor owns no deposit; he is merely a creditor of a private corporation. Most of the 'mystery' of banking would disappear as soon as a bank was no longer allowed to lend out money deposited by its customers, while, at the same time, these depositors were using that money as *their* money by drawing checks against it.

'Mr. Dooley,' the Will Rogers of his day, brought out the absurdity of this double use of money on demand deposit when he called a banker 'a man who takes care of your money by lending it out to his friends.'"[4]

While there is little doubt that the public would reap the advantages cited by Fisher the banks would be devastated by such a precipitous loss of income. Many banks already charge for the services such as cashing checks, for example, that Fisher mentioned as an alternative source of revenue. In retrospect it is little wonder that bankers were less than enthusiastic about his proposal. To go from a position of low liquidity and high earnings to one of high liquidity and low earnings was not their view of bankers' heaven.

Milton Friedman implicitly acknowledged the reality of the situation when he suggested paying the banks interest on their converted assets. This way the loss of revenue would be vastly reduced and they would, theoretically at least, be able to cope quite nicely. Certainly it would avoid the massive instability that would attach to either the Fisher or King Charles II solutions, and that is important at a time when we desperately need greater stability rather than less. It would be the people, through their government, who would pay the banks interest on their cash reserves, however, so the benefit to taxpayers would be dubious at best.

Although Friedman has not renounced his support for a 100% reserve system it is no longer on his priority list as indicated in a footnote reply to a 1983 letter from William F. Hixson. "As good a reform as ever", Friedman wrote, "... unfortunately with as little prospect of adoption as ever. I keep mentioning it but feel that tilting at windmills is not an effective way to spend my time."[5] If he had been content to let it go at that, the Nobel laureate would have earned a place among the forward-looking thinkers on a fundamentally important issue. But in subsequent writings he has recommended freezing the production of government money and the adoption of zero percent reserves.

In a 1986 letter to Professor John H. Hotson, in reply to one on the subject of reserves and government-created money, he wrote: "In my opinion, either extreme is acceptable. I have not given up advocacy of one-hundred percent reserves. I would prefer one-hundred percent reserves to the alternative I set forth. However, I believe that getting the government out of the business altogether or zero percent reserves also makes sense. The virtue of either one is that it eliminates government meddling in the lending and investing activities of the financial markets. When I wrote in 1948, we were already halfway toward one-hundred percent reserves because so large a fraction of the assets of the banks consisted of either government bonds or high-powered money. One-hundred percent reserves at that time did not look impossible of achievement. We have moved so far since then that I am very skeptical indeed that there is any political possibility of achieving one-hundred percent reserves. That does not mean that it is not desirable."[6]

Professor Friedman goes on to say that the sole reason he stressed the zero percent reserves was "because it seemed to me at least to be within the imaginable range of political feasibility."[7] He was correct on that point as two or three countries, including Canada, have already done it. But that doesn't mean it makes sense. One could argue that it is one of the worst ideas to emerge from the academy in the history of economics. What Friedman is suggesting is a system based almost exclusively on debt which is the inverted pyramid that Irving Fisher found so worrisome. It is the same inverted pyramid, grotesquely exaggerated in recent decades, which makes the present system inherently unstable. One has to be skeptical of a theory based on political expediency rather than common sense.

It is my opinion that, as of now, neither extreme is acceptable. A zero reserve system, with its incredible leverage, is not only inherently unstable it will ultimately implode with a world-shattering crash. A 100% reserve system is not really feasible either due to the size and importance of the banking industry and its need to have some revenues in addition to the growing list of fees and service charges. So it seems that a pragmatic, middle of the road course should be the order of the day – a solution that will reduce leverage to a sound level, contain the rise in the ratio of debt to GDP and still keep the banks in business.

No matter what one thinks about the banks as an industry they do perform some useful and essential functions. They are convenient places to park your money until you need it – assuming, of course, that you can get it back when you want it. The checking facilities they provide are absolutely essential to the smooth functioning of a highly-sophisticated economic system. The banks also play a role in the allocation of resources. They have done this abominably in recent years but bankers have the training and capacity to do it reasonably well if they were subject to explicit guidelines. Banks are already in place, so it would be far better to establish "rules of conduct" to ensure that money lent is consistent with the public interest than to establish competing government facilities that would be no more efficient in performing the function and, probably, much less efficient.

On the assumption, then, that a widely decentralized banking system can play an integral part in a stable system, it is both permissible and desirable to leave them with their exist-ing interest-bearing paper as a source of revenue. It is also expedient to renew or extend their licenses to "print" money (create deposits) but only to the extent that is consistent with the public interest – which should be about half of the propor-tion of new money that they have become accustomed to creating.

No one knows exactly what the split in the money-creation function would have to be to cap the debt to GDP ratio because there are too many other factors involved – especially interest rates. The 50/50 split, combined with other measures, however, would be a giant step in that direction and might, with luck, just do the job. There are no econometric programs, that I am aware of, capable of answering the question and even if there were I would be concerned about their reliability. There are, however, models which measure the impact on federal balances of a significant infusion of government-created money as well as the impact of an incomes policy on employment, growth, interest rates and inflation.

So I have had econometric simulations run for two cases to illustrate the trend lines of what is possible. The first involves only the adoption of an incomes policy along the lines of the one recommended in Chapter 10. The impact on inflation was stated in Chapter 4. Other results follow. The second case combines the incomes policy with a significant infusion of government-created money. The results, as you will see, are quite dramatic.

Opponents of government-created money insist that the policy would be inflationary. They base their case on the pretence, and it is pretence, that the reserve requirements of the banking system would remain unchanged and that the infusion of such a vast amount of high-powered money (cash) would produce an explosion in the money supply (credit) followed by inflation rampant. This is nonsense! The reserve requirements of the banks and other deposit-taking institutions would be consistently raised to the point where the total increase in the money stock – government-created money plus bank-created money – would be exactly the same as would have been the case otherwise. So the inflationary effects, if any, would not be altered. The only difference would be that the government would be printing more money and the banks would be "printing" less.

The institutional framework is important. There is, in theory at least, no reason why the Federal Reserve System couldn't be the custodian and operator of the new system provided its jurisdiction was extended to all banks as it is essential that all deposit-taking institutions be subject to the same reserve requirements. It has the advantage of being in existence and having offices (Federal Reserve Banks) in all geographical regions. An off-setting disadvantage would be the necessity of replacing most, if not all, of the Governors and senior staff. Their attitudes and utterances have been so pro-bank that they would appear to be psychologically incapable of adapting to a reformed system. Another disadvantage is that the Federal Reserve System is an expensive system!

A much better alternative would be to scrap the Fed completely and create a new Bank of the United States wholly owned by the people and staffed by committed reformers. A re-incarnated BUS would have the advantage of starting with a clean slate unencumbered by the Fed's dismal record beginning almost from the time it was created. But that is a decision only the Congress in its wisdom can make. The most important criterion is clear lines of authority and a regulatory framework that will permit fast and sensitive action.

At the beginning of each year the central bank would set up a credit in the name of the U.S. Treasury of never more than 100 percent, and never less than 50 percent of the estimated amount the money supply should grow based on the real increase in output of the economy for the previous year, adjusted for the velocity of circulation of money and any significant change in demographics or anticipated participation rates. The Treasury could issue checks against this account at the rate of one-twelfth – seasonally adjusted to accommodate the rhythm of fiscal expenditures and receipts – each month. It would then spend the money into circulation as part of its ordinary payments. To prevent excessive (inflationary) multiple creation of money on the basis of the newly-created cash money, it would probably be necessary for the central bank to raise the private banks' reserve requirements monthly in the early stages but it would have to have sufficient leeway to compensate for any unexpected changes in the velocity of circulation and other unpredictables.

In view of the long-established penchant of central bankers to maintain balanced books, the Treasury would sell the central bank common shares in the U.S. with a par value of some arbitrary amount – say $10 billion a share – which the central bank would keep on its books at cost as an asset against the "liability" of the credit or currency issued. This is preferable to the pledge of non-interest-bearing bonds which would perpetuate the upward trend of debt to GDP, because the bonds would be included in total federal debt, rather than bend the curve in the other direction.

Although the central bank should have day-to-day autonomy it should never, for obvious reasons, have absolute autonomy. Much blood was shed in getting rid of autocratic kings and our hard-won democracy, though "the worst of all possible systems", as Winston Churchill said, is still "better than all others", as he quickly added. So when it comes to monetary policy the best system would be one where the Secretary of the Treasury, as the people's representative, would be the final arbiter. The safeguard should be that any directives to the central bank would have to be in writing and would have to be made public so voters would have the information necessary to decide whether or not their interests were being well served.

As an enforcement measure the interest on loans from deposit-taking institutions would only be deductible, for tax purposes, in respect of institutions observing the reserve requirements of the U.S. central bank. That would maintain a level playing field with foreign banks making loans in U.S. dollars. If anyone were clever enough to circumvent these regulations by using non-bank third parties, for example, the interest would not only be non-deductible, but subject to a penalty tax as well.

Someone, either the central bank or the Treasury, should also have standby power over margin requirements for all kinds of credit. I will return to the subject of margins later, but here I am thinking about the power to increase minimum monthly payments on credit card balances in the event that consumer purchases began to overheat the economy; and to require higher equity to debt ratios for either residential or non-residential real-estate, or both, in case the construction industry started to bid up prices. Non-residential construction is one of the few exceptional cases where there has been demand inflation in the few cities where the banking system went berserk with its lending practices. This is a perfect example of where the brakes could have been applied in one industry, in relevant locations, without the necessity of carpet-bombing the whole economy.

Subject to these considerations, and the imposition of guidelines to limit the abuse of monopoly power which will be discussed in later chapters, it should be possible and certainly much easier to (a) balance government budgets, (b) reduce interest rates and allow the economy to grow at a faster rate while reducing debt service charges for governments and industry alike, (c) maintain price stability, i.e. annual increases in the Consumer Price Index in the order of 1 percent or less, (d) achieve a higher level of employment and (e) cap the current increase in debt to GDP ratios.

ECONOMETRIC SIMULATIONS[8]

As I mentioned in Chapter 4 these simulations begin with a "base" or "reference" case which represents the best guess consensus of a cross-section of prominent economists as to how the economy is likely to perform in the absence of any major change in policy. The model measures the impact of hypothetical policy changes as a variation from the base case.

U.S. CASE #1 – Incomes Policy Only

This exercise was designed to measure the potential impact of mandatory guidelines to limit the excesses of monopoly power by big labor and big business along the lines suggested in the next chapter. The principal advantage of wrestling inflation as near the ground as it is possible to get was spelled out in Chapter 4. The figures are repeated here for ease of reference.

Year	1996	1997	1998	1999
Gross Domestic Product:				
Base	2.2	2.0	2.0	2.7
New	2.2	2.9	3.6	3.1
Improvement	0.0	0.9	1.6	0.4
Unemployment Rate:				
Base	6.02	6.33	6.73	6.75
New	6.11	6.01	5.44	5.11
Improvement	-0.09	0.32	1.29	1.64
Consumer Price Index: (1982-84=100)				
Base	3.1	3.3	2.6	2.2
New	2.4	0.9	0.6	1.0
Improvement	0.7	2.4	2.0	1.2
Prime Rate:				
Base	9.00	8.62	7.69	7.50
New	8.30	6.29	5.61	6.27
Improvement	0.70	2.33	2.08	1.23
Federal Funds Rate:				
Base	6.01	5.61	4.62	4.40
New	5.20	3.10	2.55	3.20
Improvement	0.81	2.51	2.07	1.20
Federal Balances (Deficit):				
Base	-197	-214	-227	-234
New	-195	-178	-146	-142
Improvement	2	36	81	92

The progression of these advantages is quite straight-forward. An incomes policy which results in both lower inflation and reduced inflationary expectations makes it possible to reduce interest rates. Lower interest rates promote faster growth in interest sensitive industries resulting in more jobs, a higher GDP and increased government revenues leading to a lower deficit. Benefits all around!

U.S. CASE #2 – Incomes Policy Plus Government-Created Money

The assumptions are the same as in Case #1 but with one powerful addition. Congress is assumed to have reasserted its constitutional responsibility for the creation of money and to have decided, as a matter of practicality, to share the money-creation function with the private banks on a 50/50 ratio. This would allow a substantial infusion of debt-free money with far-reaching and highly beneficial results. The figures used for the amount of government-created money (GCM) injected into the system each year are arbitrary approximations of what the 50/50 split might produce but quite adequate for purposes of illustrating the potential.

Year	1996	1997	1998	1999
Government-Created Money ($b.)	80.0	82.5	85.0	88.0
Gross Domestic Product:				
Base	2.2	2.0	2.0	2.7
New	2.2	2.9	3.5	3.1
Improvement	0.0	0.9	1.5	0.4
Unemployment Rate:				
Base	6.02	6.33	6.73	6.75
New	6.12	6.04	5.50	5.20
Improvement	-0.10	0.29	1.23	1.55
Consumer Price Index: (1982-84=100)				
Base	3.1	3.3	2.6	2.2
New	2.4	0.9	0.6	0.9
Improvement	0.7	2.4	2.0	1.3
Prime Rate:				
Base	9.00	8.62	7.69	7.50
New	8.30	6.29	5.61	6.27
Improvement	0.70	2.33	2.08	1.23
Federal Funds Rate:				
Base	6.01	5.61	4.62	4.40
New	5.20	3.10	2.55	3.20
Improvement	0.81	2.51	2.07	1.20
Federal Balances (Deficit):				
Base	-197	-214	-227	-234
New	-113	- 92	- 54	- 45
Improvement	84	122	173	189

You will note that most of the results are not significantly different from those in Case #1. There is a modest improvement in the growth rate attributed almost exclusively to lower interest rates because no fiscal stimulation is assumed. For the same reason, despite a significant increase in the number of jobs, unemployment remains above 5%.

When similar simulations were run two years ago they showed unemployment dropping to 4% within four years. The difference is due to a considerably worsened base case reflecting an extremely gloomy view of government spending. There is no doubt that the right combination of policies could achieve an even higher growth rate and unemployment in the 4% range and what both sets of simulations have demonstrated is that the improvement can be achieved without significant inflation – the not-so-magic formula that classical economists have overlooked.

The profound difference between Case #1 and Case #2 is in the results for federal balances. The figures show that the federal deficit can be brought down within shooting distance of balance before the end of the century. In fact, with a few common sense tax changes that I will discuss later, and a little bit of fiscal stimulation in areas where it counts, federal revenues could be brought into surplus before the end of the millennium.

Again I would like to remind readers that the figures used in these exercises are not definitive. In each case they represent someone's best guess and are consequently open to challenge by those who guess differently. Their value is to indicate the impact of one set of assumptions when compared with another. So, despite the occasional anomaly, I am satisfied that the indicated trends are valid because they all correlate with common sense.

A GROWTH DIVIDEND

People sometimes ask "What will make the new government-created money good? What will give it value?" In effect it will be "made good" in exactly the same way that bank-created money is made good. The existing workforce becomes a little more efficient each year through greater knowledge and the use of better capital tools. So more goods and services are produced by the same number of people. Add to that the output from additional entrants to the workforce, whether from young people growing up or from net immigration, and you have the total increase in growth of output. So the money supply can be increased in proportion to the increase in production of real goods and services without any inflationary effects as a result. This is the essence of monetarism although the theory assumes that no one will try to grab more than their fair share which is another problem to be addressed later. For the moment we will assume "fair ball" for purposes of discussion.

The principal difference between having the government print half of the new money created each year, instead of letting the banks do it all, is that the government owns part of the increase instead of the banks. You could argue that if the government gets the money (revenue), and the people make it good, that is a form of tax. This is technically true, although I prefer to call it a growth dividend. The people finance the growth (increased output) through their government – in the role of financial intermediary – and in turn they get the benefit from the kind of services governments provide. This can be accomplished with less increase in explicit taxes which are widely regarded as high enough already. The big switch is that the people get a greater benefit from their own labor instead of working primarily for the banks which has been the over-riding result of the fractional reserve system.

The purpose of the operation is not to move to a 100% reserve system. There is no real need for theoretical purity. It is rather to increase bank reserves substantially and take away their near-monopoly on money-creation. The leverage of banks in many Western countries is positively scary and it is time to move back from the precipice of possible disaster. In addition to reducing the vulnerability of the banking system, the creation of more real money will be a move toward a safer, sounder system.

In effect it will represent a move away from such a preponderant reliance on debt in favor of a system boasting greater equity. As the volume of debt ceases to grow as rapidly, the existing debt will act as a rotating credit not too different from the way much credit is handled now. As government securities mature the proceeds will be available for re-financing. As businesses mature, and reduce their debt to equity ratios, the repayment will be available for new businesses. As people grow older, put their children through college and pay off their mortgages, the credit will be available to their children to finance the same cycle. "Crowding out" – the competition between public and private sectors for available credit – will not be affected. For every dollar the government creates it will need to borrow one dollar less. Finally, the price of money for both government and business will be more reasonable if banks are prohibited from making loans for speculative as opposed to legitimate purposes.

If this sounds like a vast improvement, it is!

THE CANADIAN CASE

The Canadian economy is almost a basket case, which means that much more heroic measures are required if our economy and our country are to survive. Our sad state can be traced directly to the effects of the last two horrendous recessions, compounded by the disrupting consequences of the North American Free Trade Agreement, rocked by political uncertainty in Quebec and exacerbated by Bank of Canada interest and exchange rate policies which have been self-defeating at best and treacherous at worst.

The monetarist philosophy has reigned supreme and without any of the redeeming qualities of common sense in its application. Our latest recession began ahead of the U.S., went deeper and lasted longer as our dogmatic Bank of Canada Governor, John Crow, relentlessly pursued his goal of price stability defined as zero inflation. We almost achieved that goal, albeit temporarily, but, as was the case with medieval doctors who bled their patients to eliminate the poison, the patient remains near death's door and in need of a massive transfusion.

As the recession deepened, and government revenues declined, deficits grew larger. But instead of allowing the Canadian banking system to finance the deficits internally our Governor kept interest rates abnormally high and encouraged foreigners to make up the shortfall. As Professor W.H. Pope wrote: "Nothing is more foolish than for a country with heavy unemployment to be a net foreign borrower. All that can be done with foreign money is buy foreign goods and services and pay interest and dividends on past capital inflows."[9] Borrowing foreign money to finance government deficits, instead of financing them internally, created employment abroad and unemployment in Canada.

These foreign currencies had to be converted into Canadian dollars to buy Canadian bonds. This increased demand for the Canadian dollar and raised it to an artificially high level – so high, in fact, that our competitive position in manufactures, resources and tourism was badly eroded. Instead of allowing us to earn our way in the world, the Governor put us deeper and deeper into debt internationally to the point where foreign bankers, instead of our government, are setting public policy. To say that our present state of affairs is the result of incredibly bad judgment on the part of Mr. Crow is the most charitable way possible of accounting for it. Five years later, in the Fall of 1995, the patient is still in intensive care, barely able to open an eyelid, and there is no orthodox treatment that will restore the pre-operative robust health.

One additional handicap was imposed when the former Governor agreed with the government of the day that it would be permissible, in the amendments to the Bank Act in 1991, to drop the provision which allowed the cabinet to set cash reserve requirements for the chartered banks. Instead the Basle Accord, authored by the Bank for International Settlement, which merely sets "risk weighted capital requirements", was adopted. Under this system government bonds are considered "risk free" and commercial loans "100% risky". A bank must have capital equal to 8% of business loans, which are considered risky, but there is no such requirement for government bonds other than the overall limitation that total assets cannot exceed 20 times capital. If this sounds complicated, it is, but the net result is a bias in favor of government debt over business requirements. The amendment of the act was requested by the banks, sponsored by the government of the day, approved either implicitly or explicitly by the Governor of the Bank of Canada, and allowed to pass without serious debate by an opposition which was oblivious of the potentially disastrous consequences.

After achieving near zero inflation in 1994, Canada adopted a reasonable interest rate policy – nominal rates comparable to U.S. rates, though real rates were still considerably higher – which had just begun to promote modest growth when the 1994 barrage from the Fed was launched. Monetarist policy has a very different effect in the U.S. and Canada. In the U.S. most homeowners have 15 to 30 year mortgages so if the Fed raises interest rates they are not immediately affected. The change applies primarily to those about to purchase a house and those borrowing for business activities.   In Canada, a substantial proportion of home mortgages are short-term. Consequently, when interest rates go up, a huge number of people who already own homes are hit, as well as new home buyers. Thus the same monetarist policy affects consumer confidence and spending much more in Canada than in the U.S. For Canadian business loans the increase is at least tax deductible whereas for mortgages it is after tax income, which makes the hit even more drastic. (Mortgage payments are not tax-deductible in Canada.) In both countries of course, higher interest rates increase the cost of servicing government debt.

If the cash reserve requirement had remained in place the Bank of Canada could have purchased Canadian bonds to keep nominal rates from rising in concert with U.S. rates. With inflation almost 3 percentage points less than U.S. inflation, there was some maneuvring room. But the ability to pursue an independent interest-rate policy, consistent with an independent inflation policy, was effectively lost when there was no way to sterilize the massive infusion of high-powered money that would have gone into the system. As a result real Canadian long-term interest rates soared above 9 percent, and in the Fall of 1995 remain well above 6% which is more than double the historic rate. Needless to say, the extra, unanticipated cost of servicing the debt played havoc with the government's budgetary predictions.

The very first move Canada must take, then, is to revise the Bank Act one more time and make provision for cash reserve ratios as determined by the government or by the Bank of Canada on its behalf. Once that has been done the government will be in a position to begin the massive stimulation that is required to reduce the level of unemployment from the current 9.4% (Oct. '95) to something more morally and economically acceptable.

As the Canadian situation is so much more desperate, both economically and politically, than in the U.S. and as repeated simulations have demonstrated the positive benefits of an incomes policy on growth, employment and interest rates, I am just including one simulation for Canada which combines an incomes policy with a massive injection of government-created money. The combined objectives are increased expenditure by government to stimulate growth, substantial tax reductions for the same purpose, and, at the same time, elimination of the federal deficit in accordance with the dictates of the financial market. Increased expenditures would be directed to health care, education, environmental protection and the reinstatement of essential government services to levels consistent with public safety and good management. Increased expenditures by consumers would result from the elimination of the Goods and Services Tax, over a three year period, without replacing it with any other tax.

THE CANADIAN CASE – An Incomes Policy Plus Government-Created Money

Year	1996	1997	1998	1999
Direct Stimulation by Gov't C$b.	10.0	12.5	15.0	10.0
Stim. from Tax Reductions C$b.	6.1	12.5	19.2	20.0
Total Tax & Cash Stim. C$b.	16.1	25.0	34.2	30.0
Infusion of Government-Created Money C$b.	10.0	17.5	25.0	22.5

Year	1996	1997	1998	1999
Gross Domestic Product: (% Increase)				
Base	1.6	2.0	2.4	2.5
New	5.7	4.1	4.1	1.8
Improvement	4.1	2.1	1.7	-0.7
Unemployment Rate: (%)				
Base	9.77	9.75	9.65	9.30
New	6.98	5.75	4.48	5.00
Improvement	2.79	4.00	5.17	4.30
Consumer Price Index: (Year-over-Year % Change)				
Base	1.6	1.7	2.0	2.0
New	0.5	-0.2	0.1	1.6
Improvement	1.1	1.9	1.9	0.4
Corporate Long-Term Bond Yield:				
Base	8.52	8.21	7.93	7.78
New	7.77	6.98	6.46	6.62
Improvement	0.75	1.23	1.47	1.16
Housing Starts: (000's)				
Base	142	154	155	155
New	150	163	162	161
Improvement	8	9	7	6
Federal Government Balances C$b.:				
Base	-13.5	-8.2	-5.3	-1.4
New	-8.0	1.9	7.8	11.1
Improvement	5.5	10.1	13.1	12.5
All Government Balances (Federal & Provincial) C$b.:				
Base	-23.3	-17.6	-13.5	-8.5
New	-15.0	-1.2	10.4	16.9
Improvement	8.3	16.4	23.9	25.4
Total Federal Government Debt C$b.:				
Base	502.9	515.6	527.5	533.0
New	497.2	499.3	497.4	489.8
Improvement	5.7	16.3	30.1	43.2
Total Provincial Government Debt:				
Base	313.6	328.9	343.1	354.9
New	316.8	330.5	338.4	338.3
Improvement	-3.2	-1.6	4.7	16.6

The results of this simulation are marvellously exciting. Three years of powerful economic growth would reduce unemployment to near moral levels, that is to 5% or less because the official figure of 9.4% at the end of October, 1995, is slightly below the 9.77% base case used for the simulation. This could be accomplished with negligible inflation. The imposition of the incomes policy guarantees low core inflation. On top of that is the one time benefit from eliminating the much hated Goods and Services Tax. This disastrous tax has been a thorn in the side of both business and consumers as well as a genuine irritant to tourists from the U.S. and abroad. Its elimination would be cause for national celebration.

While the provision of jobs and the re-establishment of hope would be a great moral victory the economic results are equally profound. Within two years the federal budget would go from deficit to surplus. Within three years the combined federal and provincial budgets would move from deficit to surplus. In less than three years the federal government debt would cease to rise and would then begin to fall. The same would be true for provincial governments but it would take a year longer. The trump card is that a combination of lower interest rates and higher revenues, due to higher employment and increased output, would permit both federal and provincial governments to cap their debt both as a percentage of GDP and in absolute terms. It has to happen for the country to survive and the simulations show that it could be done quickly if we put the accelerator right to the floorboard just as we would in a shooting war. The good news is that if we showed the same ingenuity and common sense to win the peace as we did to win the war a country which is currently on the ropes would soon be a land of opportunity once more.

CONCLUSION

A few conclusions can be reached from the U.S. and Canadian simulations. First, notwithstanding all the hokus-pokus about the Phillips Curve and the "natural" rate of unemployment, it is quite possible to achieve acceptable levels of unemployment and inflation simultaneously and for the long run. This is of primary importance! Then, with reasonable expenditure and taxation policies, it is possible to balance budgets at all levels of government. Finally, by splitting the money-creation function, the leverage of the banking system can be reduced to a sane and sound level and the worrisome upward trend in debt to GDP ratios for both governments and the economy at large capped before they become even more oppressive.

CHAPTER 10

AN INCOMES POLICY FOR MONOPOLIES AND OLIGOPOLIES

"All the forces in the world are not as powerful as an idea whose time has come."

Victor Hugo

The simulations in the previous chapter indicate quite clearly that higher levels of growth can be sustained under the protective umbrella of an incomes policy that keeps the monopoly power of big business and big labor in check. It is a climate in which the economic system should work well all of the time instead of just some of the time. The goal is the simultaneous achievement of full employment and stable prices not just temporarily but for an extended period.

This is where monetarism has failed. It has an incomes policy aspect to the extent that it is designed to slow down or stop excessive wage and price gains. Unfortunately, its means of doing so is both cruel and inefficient. Despite the damage caused by its policies, price stability has never been achieved! Also, to the extent it has been responsible for reducing inflation, this has never been for an extended period. Of the many incomes policies I have looked at, including earlier American and Canadian experiments, monetarism is, unquestionably, the worst!

I am in total agreement with the goal of price stability. Eliminating inflation is critically important because any inflation is too much. Inflation is a form of larceny. It robs one group of people (lenders) for the benefit of another group (borrowers). Having said that, if I thought that "hard money" could only be achieved at the expense of the poor and the unemployed, then my vote would be for the disadvantaged, on the basis that people are of greater value than money. But it is my belief that the trade-off theory, in the extremes to which it is widely accepted, is as phony as a $3 bill.

Certainly there is a level of unemployment at which demand for labor would begin to increase the price. But that is not the same level of unemployment which would trigger higher union demands in contract negotiations in the course of an economic recovery. The latter is a much higher "unnatural" rate which the monetarists have labeled "natural" because it sounds better than the reality which is "high unemployment". So the debate between those who contend that the economy has changed so fundamentally that inflation is no longer a threat and those who fear that too much stimulation would pour fuel on the dying embers is really a joke. As Fed chairman Alan Greenspan told the Economic Club of Chicago in October, 1995, "We have to be careful not to lull ourselves into the presumption that somehow the institutional structure of the American economy and its increasing globalization is permanently suppressing inflation."[1]

Indeed we cannot. Six times since I first entered public life central banks have chosen to curb inflation by means of tightening the money supply and raising interest rates. Each time inflation has been temporarily reduced: and always, when restraint has been relaxed, wage settlements and inflation have begun to rise again. There is no reason to believe that anything has changed other than a longer period of tight money and correspondingly slow growth. Workers, increasingly frustrated by the extended malaise, will seize the first practical opportunity to catch up and move ahead – especially when they read about increases in executive compensation and compare it with their own. Regrettably an overly aggressive initiative by labor would only lead to renewed inflation and another monetary crackdown so alternative means of achieving real wage gains must be found. Fortunately, a large dose of common sense will allow us to have our cake and eat it too. To achieve price stability, however, we must achieve stable labor unit costs. And that is not practical in a full employment environment in the absence of an effective incomes policy to prevent the abuse of market power.

There is so much at stake. Consider a riddle. What do the provision of jobs for people who want to work, affordable housing for people who need homes, reduced carrying charges on the national debt, cheaper electricity, relief for farmers and a break for the Third World have in common? The answer? Lower interest rates! Why are current interest rates both so much more erratic and so much higher than they were 25 years ago? It is primarily due to inflation and the fear of inflation in conjunction with the deliberate policy of the Fed to use interest rates as its principal tool in damping wage-push inflation. There has to be, and is, a better way of wrestling inflation to the ground, and the unsustainable level of high interest rates with it.

INCENTIVE INDEXING

Incentive indexing is the most appropriate way to describe my proposed incomes policy with its limited but essential objective. It is not to be mistaken for any system of comprehensive wage and price controls because it is not comparable. It is simply an antidote to the special immunities already granted to labor unions and a complement to antitrust and anticombines laws that are quite impotent to cope with the peculiar characteristics of oligopolistic industry. It prescribes rules designed to prevent the abuse of power while at the same time encouraging both business and labor to enjoy the benefits of increased efficiency and the resulting higher real incomes.

There is little point in submitting to a disastrous recession and then sitting idly by and watching the inflationary spiral begin afresh a few months later. As the Fed tacitly admits when it raises interest rates, the market power of big business and big unions, which gave rise to the problem, will not have disappeared in the interim. The 17-month strike of the Caterpillar company by the United Auto Workers which ended when the union capitulated in late 1995 showed that union power is not as great as it once was; but if the economy were stimulated to its potential the bargaining power of big labor would still be a limiting factor. Consequently, some kind of incomes policy is necessary to act as a permanent "temperature control" to keep wages and prices from exploding.

Unfortunately, the record of success of incomes policies to date is not a happy one; thus many experts dismiss the idea except for use in emergencies. Still there are economists who seem to share my conviction that past failures are attributable to a combination of careless design and inconsistent application rather than to the concept itself. Arthur Burns, former Chairman of the Board of Governors of the Federal Reserve System, with whom I discussed the problem on more than one occasion, once told me that an incomes policy is the only solution. "Governments will continue to experiment with incomes policies," he said, "they will apply them, then take them off again; try again and then backtrack, until somebody, somewhere, eventually gets it right."[2] Burns knew from first-hand experience that monetary policy and monopoly power mix like gas and water.

There have been a variety of experiments to date and while some were quite successful for extended periods they eventually failed for predictable reasons. Many were voluntary and consequently were doomed from the outset. Others had bureaucrats establishing wages and prices – a system which has never worked except briefly during an emergency such as war-time. Still others distributed the benefits of technology on the basis of specific industries which was both unfair and seen to be unfair. Inevitably the practice led to failure and abandonment.

In the United States, the *Annual Report of the President's Council of Economic Advisers* set out criteria for both unions and management in 1962. The concept received general support for a few years, when it enjoyed a protective umbrella of civic responsibility. But by 1966 public discipline had pretty well evaporated, and whether the breakdown resulted from the Vietnam War or simply bigger wage demands is, in a sense, irrelevant. The lid on prices was effectively blown.

In August 1971 President Nixon confounded the experts by reversing his policy and introducing compulsory controls. Prices, incomes and dividends were frozen for ninety days while spot checks were undertaken to ensure compliance. Phase Two was a period of tight controls following the freeze. Price stability during this period was encouraging – so much so, in fact, that Mr. Nixon moved on to Phase Three, which meant a return to voluntary controls. It didn't take long thereafter for conditions to return to "normal", with the whole plan being abandoned.

President Carter's October 1978 initiative launched "a program of price and pay standards designed to brake the price-wage spiral that has beset our economy for more than a decade."[3] His voluntary program included an explicit numerical ceiling for wage and fringe benefits, as well as a price deceleration standard for individual firms.

In January 1979 the President's Council underlined the difficulty with voluntary plans: "One of the obstacles to the success of voluntary wage and price standards is fear on the part of each group of workers that their observance of the wage standard could lead to a loss of real income if others do not cooperate, or if uncontrollable events, such as a serious crop shortage, result in price increases. Faced with such uncertainty and basing their price expectations on recent patterns of inflation, any workers might be reluctant to cooperate with the standards program. To improve the acceptability of the standards, the Administration is proposing to the Congress an innovative program of real wage insurance for those who observe them."[4]

Unfortunately, Congress did not pass the real wage insurance law as requested by the President. Furthermore, the courts rejected the legality of a system that lacked legislative authority.[5] So the guidelines remained voluntary in the literal sense.

"Studies by the Council of Economic Advisers reinforce the view that the President's program aided in keeping wage rates from accelerating.... However, both the employment cost index for union workers, and the effective wage change in collective bargaining units covering 1,000 workers or more, showed a greater increase in the 4 quarters through September 1979 than in the preceding 4 quarters."[6] At the same time productivity decreased and labor unit costs jumped by 11.3 percent, compared with 7 or 8 percent over the same four quarters a year earlier.[7]

No lesson from past experience could be clearer than the observation that voluntary systems are essentially useless except for very brief periods at a time of acknowledged national crisis. To reinforce this conclusion, I have often asked audiences what their attitude would be if income tax was voluntary. Would they pay more, the same, or less tax than now required by law? Usually a couple of altruists insist that they would pay the same; but the overwhelming majority admit honestly that they would remit considerably less if the amount were open to their discretion.

The principle is straightforward. Most people will obey laws that appear to be just if they are fairly enforced. But they will also take advantage of any concessions, opportunities, privileges, or even loopholes permitted by the law. In the words of that great nineteenth-century liberal John Stuart Mill, "the interference of law is required, not to overrule the judgement of individuals but to give effect to that judgement: they being unable to give effect to it except by concert, which concert again cannot be effectual unless it receives validity and sanction from the law."[8]

GUIDELINES NOT REQUIRED IN THE MARKET SECTOR

If an incomes policy must be mandatory to be effective, the next question that arises is whether or not it should apply to the whole economy. And, if not, what segments should be exempt? The day that President Nixon's wage and price freeze was invoked in August 1971, I predicted that the controls would

ultimately fail because they were attempting the impossible –
never a sound foundation for economic policy. My objection
was based on two factors: first, the inclusion of commodities,
especially food; second, the simplistic treatment of the economy
as one animal, without regard to the dichotomy between the
market and oligopolistic sectors.[9]

Because I was raised on a farm, and one of my first
business ventures was marketing fruit, I was particularly
sensitive on the first point. I recalled how quickly prices
changed in response to supply and demand. Strawberries were
an extreme case. A price set early in the season, when the
berries first appeared, would be unrealistically high a week
later. Similarly, a price set in mid-season would be far too low
in early or late season, when supplies were scarce. The same
problem applied to a lesser extent with other foods and many
internationally traded commodities. While it is easy to pass
regulations attempting to control prices in these cases, it is not
easy to enforce them when they don't make sense in light of
market conditions.

Just as it is impossible to effectively control the prices
of commodities, which fluctuate with changing supply and
demand, it is not necessary to impose controls where genuine
market conditions exist. If it is theoretically possible for
monetary policy to regulate prices in a free market economy,
then it should be possible to regulate that part of the economy
which is genuinely "free". One does not need to interfere with
the market where the market actually governs.

The problem, as I explained earlier, is not the market.
It is the fact that the "free" or market sector is frustrated in its
operation by wage and price leadership from the sector that is,
by definition, rigid. The economy is like two horses tied to the
same wagon. The stronger horse – the one with market power
– pulls out in front. So instead of a team, you have a lead
horse getting out of line and tending to pull the wagon around
in circles. A steady pull requires either an inflationary
monetary policy, so that the laggard can keep up, or a tether
on the lead horse.

The object of an essential incomes policy, then, is to control labor unit costs in the rigid sector and then to ensure that the benefits of increased productivity are shared by all members of society. Stated as a principle, the function of an incomes policy is to do the job that antitrust and anticombines laws were intended to do, have failed to do, and never can do. It is to keep the monopolies and oligopolies, the powerful lead horse, in harness with the rest of the economy so that the whole can move forward together.

There is bound to be some difference of opinion as to who should be subject to regulation and who should not. Generally speaking, guidelines should apply to all monopolies, oligopolies, and cartels – all cases of "less than perfect" market conditions. This view has been expressed by others, including J.K. Galbraith, who has long promoted the concept.[10]

There will always be borderline cases where it is not entirely clear whether an industry is oligopolistic or not, so it should be possible for each company or industry to opt either for the free or the controlled sector. When a company or industry opts in favor of the regulated sector, it should have the protection of the law with regard to prices. That means that it would be exempt from anticombines law in respect of pricing, and that the public interest would be protected by observance of the profit guidelines laid down in the incomes policy.

When, on the other hand, a company or industry chooses in favor of the free and uncontrolled sector it must, in fact, compete in respect to prices as well as in other areas. Should there be any evidence of price fixing, identical bidding, or lack of genuine competition at any time, the choice should be subject to appeal. The public interest must be given the benefit of the doubt.

Official recognition of the existence and legitimacy of oligopolies would not eliminate the necessity for public review of mergers and takeovers. But observance of guidelines set by an incomes policy should relieve officers and directors of companies from the threat of going to jail for doing what comes naturally.

On the labor side, all collective agreements should be assumed to be monopolistic in nature and subject to the policy. Of course there are cases where this is not literally true. Small unions have been broken and non-union labor hired. But for all practical purposes the big unions do constitute a monopoly labor supply. Trying to differentiate between the big unions that do constitute a monopoly and the little ones that might not is too difficult and conducive to acrimony. So there is no simpler test, nor one easier to administer; a collective agreement, by definition, must be subject to the policy.

WHO SETS PRICES AND WAGES?

One final question remains. If big business and organized labor should be subject to an incomes policy, who should set the individual prices and wages? Looking for the answer takes us back to earlier experiments, including wartime experience. Almost everyone who was then involved in controlling prices is against the reimposition of controls. But why? Controls did seem to work for some time under emergency conditions when there was widespread public support for them. But later, anomalies appeared that led to black markets and other arrangements of convenience.

As always, the original prices had been those previously set by the trade. But as costs went up, and profit margins were squeezed, there was no quick, effective way to cope. Even when it was permissible for extra costs to be "passed through", the bureaucratic machinery was too cumbersome to avoid unacceptable delays. So businesses adopted survival tactics of cutting quality, taking under-the-table payments, or removing the product from the market altogether.

Even when control prices are set by "experts", the results are likely to be unsatisfactory. An example from my own experience in the housing business is illustrative. To encourage the production of houses to meet the desperate post-war shortage, the Canadian government had its agency, the Central (now Canada) Mortgage and Housing Corporation, insure high-ratio mortgage loans. For a builder to qualify, however, the CMHC retained the right to set the retail price of the house.

By the early '50s the market had eased to the point where, in many cases, the government's maximum price had become a convenient "minimum". Sellers confronted buyers with the fact that the asking price had been set by the government and in this way used the official figures to sustain prices higher than would have been set by the market. It was an inflexible system, however, so several builders consulted the responsible minister about removing the controls. Inevitably, the reply from CMHC was always highly negative; price-setting would continue.

A builder myself, I volunteered to produce my company's cost sheets, which showed profit margins ranging from minus $400 to plus $1,900 a unit on the basis of the controlled prices.[11] Obviously, there was no incentive to build the unprofitable models, so purchasers were restricted in their choice. The minister through whom the CMHC reported to parliament, Bob Winters, was impressed, and two weeks later the controls were removed. Within a month new house prices in Toronto had fallen an average of $400 each.

In all the experiments with price controls and incomes policies to date, there is no case where a bureaucratic machine has been able to set prices quickly enough and accurately enough to be acceptable. It is my opinion that a bureaucratic structure could never do so; its expertise is too limited and its data too stale. Governments simply should not get involved in the business of price-fixing. They should opt, instead, for mandatory profit guidelines, an alternative that eliminates the possibility of black-marketeering and of product substitution or restriction for the purpose of circumventing regulations.

Experience has shown the "order of magnitude" of the long-term return on capital associated with each industry. No single formula need apply. Guidelines could be devised that would accommodate the special requirements of different types of industries and conglomerates and still leave them the autonomy required for successful operation.

There would have to be a provision to allow profit-averaging over some reasonable period, say four years. It would be unfair, as well as unworkable, to require compliance in each calendar or fiscal year. Industry is faced with too many variables to alter course abruptly, and needs the flexibility to permit long-range planning.

Sensible guidelines would have no effect on investment. New, entrepreneurial companies would be exempt because they are invariably competitive. Guidelines would only apply to mature, oligopolistic industry, and in more than 95 percent of cases the allowable profit would be well in excess of anything companies have been able to achieve in recent years.

I have avoided specific figures because the purpose of this book is to discuss principles without getting bogged down in controversy over whether a specific industry should be allowed a maximum of 15 or 20 percent return on invested capital. But in all cases the guidelines would be more than adequate to maintain investor interest.

For the same reasons that government is not qualified to set individual prices, it should avoid getting involved in setting individual wages. The bureaucratic machinery required would bog down hopelessly. Not only that, it would just be a duplication of the existing facilities available to management and labor. So government should limit itself to the determination of an over-all wage guideline based on the previous year's increase in real output per member of the labor force adjusted to reflect any redistribution of income, either domestic, such as pay equity, or external, such as a big hike in oil prices, that might have to be taken into account.

Once the figure has been set, adjustments to individual wages and salaries should be made through direct management-labor channels. The only overriding criterion must be that the total package, including fringe benefits and wage drift[12] - a general job reclassification that results in higher average pay - does not exceed the limit set by the policy. This doesn't mean that no one would ever get an increase greater than the guideline. Privates would still be promoted to corporal, and corporals to sergeant. Line workers would become section heads and earn the raise consistent with their increased responsibilities. This is all provided for in the system. Only an attempt to accelerate the tempo of promotion for the sole purpose of cheating on the guidelines would destroy their effect and consequently would be prohibited.

AVERAGE WAGE INCREASES MUST EQUAL AVERAGE PRODUCTIVITY GAINS

The reason the wage guideline must be based on the average increase in real output is because there is such a vast range of productivity rates between earth-moving, petro-chemicals and manufacturing, for example, on the high end of the scale, and some of the service industries like education and health care on the low end. In these latter cases productivity, as we measure it, may be zero or even negative when more doctors and nurses are required for a complicated operation or when the number of students per teacher is reduced in order to provide more time with each.

It would be unjust and unworkable, to give workers in high productivity industries big increases and those in many service industries no increase at all. Indeed, in the several jurisdictions where this has been tried the system has failed miserably. Taking an average is the only way that both justice and price stability can be achieved. The cost of some services, where the guideline exceeds productivity increases, will rise. The cost (price) of most manufactures, where wage increases are less than productivity increases, should come down. Lower prices for manufactured products will offset higher prices for services and in this way price stability will be achieved.

PROFIT SHARING

Although union wages would be indexed to average productivity increases, and this tractor-trailer relationship should be sufficient incentive for everyone to pull together to increase output, a powerful case can be made for allowing profit-sharing agreements as an added bonus. I personally would both permit and encourage collective agreements providing for a bonus to workers of some modest percentage of a company's pre-tax profits – through either direct or deferred profit-sharing plans.

This idea was promoted by the late Walter Reuther when he was President of the United Auto Workers. It was not popular with management at the time, but as the years pass it is being recognized as the type of concession whereby corporations have little to lose and much to gain. Executives award themselves bonuses for producing results and there is no reason why the principle shouldn't apply to everyone involved. There is, after all, nothing like a work force with a direct incentive to be productive.

Workers would gain on both fronts. First directly, as their company prospered, and then through higher wages as better individual results contributed to a higher national average of increased efficiency. There would be a strong incentive to establish joint management-labor productivity councils in each bargaining unit because everyone would benefit from the results of initiative and imagination. Improved performance in thousands of individual bargaining units would soon add up to a measurable increase in the national guidelines.

ARBITRATING GRIEVANCES

One other point involves the internal redistribution of income referred to earlier. It is inevitable, whenever an incomes policy is applied, that some group or class of workers would be caught at a disadvantage. This cannot be avoided, and the best that can be done is to establish a body to hear grievances and arbitrate claims for catch-up. This task might be assigned to a wage board appointed exclusively, or at least predominantly, from the ranks of trade unions. The board would hear and evaluate complaints and decide how much catch-up, if any, was justified and the time frame over which it would be allowed.

All awards of this kind would have to fit within the total sum provided by law and excluded from general distribution. In other words, the general guideline would be a little bit less than the average increase in output for the previous year so that there would be a small pool available for the cases of catch-up – at least in the early years until the most blatant distortions had been ironed out.

ENFORCEMENT

Enforcement of all wage and profit guidelines would be effected by means of the income and corporations tax laws. A schedule of profit guidelines would be incorporated at the outset and amended only if experience proved that they were too restrictive. The wages guideline would be amended each year to reflect the average productivity increase for the previous year and while it would not apply to non-union labor it would give all employers a clear indication of what would be inflationary and what would not.

Using the existing tax laws is the simplest and most efficient method of enforcement because the Internal Revenue System in the United States and Revenue Canada in Canada are well equipped for the task and no expensive new bureaucracy is required. Excess wage and profit increases would simply be taxed at 100 percent, with additional penalties for cases of deliberate non-compliance.

This is not the place to set out the specifics of an incomes policy. The staff work involved should be undertaken in partnership by government, management, and labor. Not only is any system more likely to be acceptable if it is developed in a spirit of cooperation, but early private sector involvement should guarantee the avoidance of many pitfalls.

Even then, some minor flaws are to be expected. The late Arthur Burns would likely have agreed that the probability of developing a "perfect system" is too remote to be taken seriously. Like Marx's long-awaited withering away of the state, the notion of an earthly Utopia will remain a will-o'-the-wisp as long as there are people involved. The most we can hope for is a system that avoids some of the grievous errors associated with previous experiments and embodies principles compatible with the real economic environment in which it would be applied.

THE TIP: AN ALTERNATIVE?

I have tried to incorporate all the significant lessons from past experience into the design of a better system. Still, I am sure someone will wonder if I have considered the merits of alternative ideas such as the concept of a tax-based incomes policy (TIP) as proposed by Wallach & Weintraub and endorsed by *The New York Times* in a lead editorial in 1983.[13]

A tax-based incomes policy is one that can either reward workers for limiting pay increases to a prescribed level or penalize them if they don't. Similarly companies could be rewarded for limiting price increases to an established guideline or penalized for non-compliance. It is very different from my formula in its breadth of application and the complexity of operation.

The 1981 *Annual Report of the President's Council of Economic Advisers* discusses tax-based incomes policies at some length: "Several choices must be made in designing a TIP. First, should it dispense rewards or levy penalties? Second, should receiving the penalty or reward depend only on being above or below the standard (a 'hurdle' TIP), or should the size of the penalty or reward be graduated in accordance with the difference between the standard and the actual pay or price increase (a 'continuous' TIP)? Third, should the TIP apply to pay, to prices, or to both? These choices require striking a balance among equity, efficiency, administrative ease and effectiveness in reducing inflation."[14]

The Council concludes: "For several reasons, a reward pay TIP is probably preferable to a penalty pay TIP." This would cost a substantial amount in forgone revenues (tax credits), however, so "a reward TIP would only be feasible when tax cuts were being considered.... A TIP limited to a few thousand large firms with computerized personnel records would have much smaller public and private administrative costs than a TIP that included millions of small firms." But this "would be vigorously opposed by workers in small firms, who would argue, rightly, that they were being deprived of a potential tax cut."[15]

The final major issue, the Council suggests, is whether a TIP should be permanent or temporary. "The answer seems to be that a permanent TIP would not be feasible because of the distortions it would create by discouraging changes in relative wages. A TIP might introduce further distortions as people changed their behavior to circumvent the intent of the policy while remaining technically in compliance with the standard."[16]

"On balance", concluded the Council, "a temporary hurdle TIP – a tax credit to groups of workers whose average pay increase does not exceed a specified standard – seems superior to other variants." This would probably have to be coupled with a price TIP for political reasons "because restraints on pay alone, even with a reward TIP, might appear inequitable." The Council estimated that for a cost of $12 billion its temporary, voluntary system might reduce wage inflation by .79 to .93 percent, depending on the pay standard set. For $16 billion, an improvement of .91 to 1.09 percent might be expected.[17]

To impose such a complicated system for such a small benefit seems to me a little bit ridiculous. The plan fails to recognize either the permanent nature of the power and influence of monopolies and oligopolies or the likelihood that the wage-price spiral would resume its upward trend when the TIP was abandoned. A TIP, in my opinion, would be just another temporary expedient, which, like President Carter's voluntary scheme, might be better than nothing, but not much better.

It is axiomatic that stable prices are impossible without constant labor unit costs. Therefore it follows that inflation will exit permanently only with an incentive-indexed incomes policy that deals forcibly and realistically with the structural effects of monopoly power. To do this it must (a) be mandatory, (b) be permanent, (c) apply only to the rigid sector of the economy, and (d) allow companies and their unions to set their own prices and wages within the parameters set down by the policy.

ACHIEVING A CONSENSUS

Often when I speak on this subject people will say: "It sounds good, but you will never get big business and big labor to agree." Without underestimating the extent of the selling job to be done, I respectfully disagree. I would never propose a policy that I believed to be beyond the realm of practical politics. In addition, I have delivered literally hundreds of lectures on the subject and the acceptance rate of the audiences – people who say "Why don't we try it?" – has always been between 60% and 70%, and there has been little difference between union and non-union audiences. The same level of support has been registered in radio and television polls.

I will never forget one particular experience when I was giving my spiel on television. Half-way through the program I suddenly realized that the cameramen were all union members and I was concerned as to what they might be thinking. I decided to play it cool and kept going. At the end of the program all three came up to chat and to assure me that what I had been saying, in their opinion, made a lot of sense. One of them even said: "Mr. Hellyer, I would buy a used car from you" which I considered one of the better compliments of my political career.

This experience simply confirmed that the average person is no fool and if you give people the facts the majority will be persuaded, because the arithmetic is simple. For 27 years U.S. workers produced 0.8% more goods and services, on average, than they did the year before (see Table 2, Page 34). If that trend were to continue everyone could have an annual wage increase of 0.8% without increasing labor unit costs and subsequently prices. When anyone gets more than the average increase in real output it is either at someone else's expense (a redistribution of income) or, if the Fed permits an increase in the money stock to accommodate the bigger wage gains, a contribution to inflation.

That is what happened for the 27 years from 1964-1991. Wage increases averaged 6% which resulted in average inflation of 5.2% – representing the difference between real output and nominal wage gains initiated by monopoly power and made possible by increases in the money stock. The illusive gains of high nominal increases were of no benefit to labor, however, because Figure 13 demonstrates very clearly that real wages are tied directly to real output and bear no relationship to nominal wages. Obviously workers have nothing to lose and much to gain from accepting settlements based on real increases in output. In fact that is the most likely way to increase overall productivity and real wage gains.

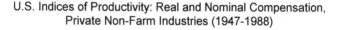

U.S. Indices of Productivity: Real and Nominal Compensation,
Private Non-Farm Industries (1947-1988)

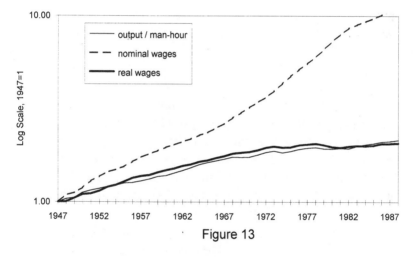

Figure 13

Source: *U.S. Monthly Labour Review,* 1989

The second reason for acceptance is that for the country as a whole there is no other choice. Interest rates must come down. If they don't, even the strongest of nations, the United States, will be brought to its economic knees. Figure 14 illustrates how the debt burden will increase over time without a dramatic change in policy. As I pointed out in Chapter 1, the figures chosen for rates of growth in GDP at 2.5% and interest on the total debt of 6.25% were purely arbitrary; but the trend isn't. The trend is real! Projecting 50 years into the future from the 1994 figures of $6.736 trillion GDP and $12.970 trillion total public and private debt,[18] the trend indicates that the United States is headed for its biggest economic crisis ever.

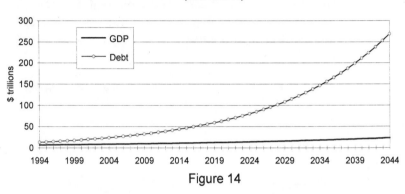

Projection of U.S. Debt Growing at 6.25 % and GDP at 2.5 %
(1994-2044)

Figure 14

Figures 15 and 16 give an indication of the extent to which the gap between the growth of GDP and total public and private debt could be narrowed through changes in public policy. Figure 15 projects an increase in the growth rate from 2½ to 3 percent and a reduction in average interest rates from 6.25 percent to 5 percent. The gap is still of crisis proportion.

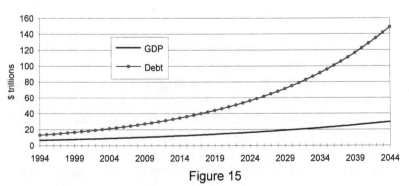

Projection of U.S. Debt Growing at 5 % and GDP at 3 %
(1994-2044)

Figure 15

Figure 16 projects a further increase in the growth rate from 3 percent to 3½ percent which is comparable to that of the '50s and '60s. The interest rate remains at an average 5 percent. The 50 year projection shows that the gap between income and debt is still untenable. Obviously other measures, including monetary reform, are required to cap the debt/GDP ratio. Equally obvious is the absolute necessity of achieving the lowest interest rate possible compatible with the lowest inflation rate possible – a rate which can only be achieved with an incomes policy.

Projection of U.S. Debt Growing at 5 % and GDP at 3.5 %
(1994-2044)

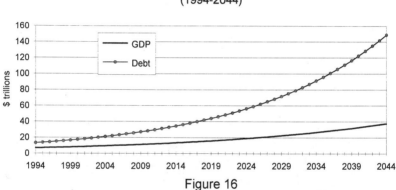

Figure 16

SUMMARY

In spite of the facts, there will be business and union leaders who resist change. One top union official told me: "Of course you're right, but we'll fight you in the trenches." I have no doubt of that and I suspect that one of the most comic aspects of any campaign would be the sight of union leaders and bank presidents on the same platform defending "free enter-prise" and "free collective bargaining" with all the intense sincerity that would be justified if access to banking and unions was really free and unrestricted. In the end their view would not and could not prevail, however, because it would be under-mined by the good sense of the majority for whom they presum-ed to speak. A greater impediment is the refusal of politicians to lead. The majority of the ones I talk to are totally petrified at the thought of initiating and proclaiming the necessity for major change even in the face of impending disaster.

CHAPTER 11

SOME MYTHS AND REALITIES
OF ECONOMICS

"Everything's got a moral, if you can only find it."

Lewis Carroll

I have argued that monetary reform and an incomes policy to curb the power of monopolies and oligopolies are two essential reforms if capitalism is to survive and prosper. There are other reforms of varying degrees of importance, but before going on to discuss them I would like to take time out for a very brief review of economic history since the industrial revolution and a quick peek at some of the philosophical questions that influence economic thought.

A Few Points of Economic History

- The industrial revolution changed for all time the order of magnitude of the potential for increased production of goods.
- No one designed a system to increase the money supply at a rate proportional to the increased output of goods.
- Banks already existed in some countries so they assumed the monetary role by default.

- A monetary system where bank deposits were backed partly, but not wholly, by gold evolved and grew like topsy. It was called a fractional reserve system of banking.
- Under the gold standard, total bank credit varied wildly as gold moved out of the country to pay for imports or into the country in payment for exports.
- The creation of credit (money), consequently, was usually either too much or too little – rarely just the right amount to promote non-inflationary economic growth.
- The periodic inflations and deflations of bank credit caused booms and busts.
- The boom-bust cycle led to a political division between those who defended the status quo and those who believed a better system should be possible.
- Laymen blamed a periodic shortage of purchasing power for the mass unemployment which occurred during each bust or depression.
- Economists said this was impossible and recited Jean Baptiste Say's Law to the effect that all production creates an equal and opposite demand and consequently there could be no such thing as a periodic shortage of purchasing power.
- One hundred and fifty years after the industrial revolution John Maynard Keynes said that of course there was a periodic shortage of purchasing power and when that situation occurred governments should borrow money to stimulate the economy and then pay it off during boom times.
- The gold standard was always abandoned during wartime when rapid monetary expansion was essential. When the war was over economic theorists would demand a return to the gold standard – usually at the pre-war parity.
- Capitalism prospered in good times but faltered badly when monetary crises occurred such as the one that precipitated the Great Depression of the 1930s.

- Most economists, failing to recognize the problem, recommended in 1932 that the federal government should reduce its deficit and balance its budget.
- There were exceptions like F.H. Knight, L.W. Mints, Henry Schultz, H.C. Simons, G.V. Cox, Aaron Director, Paul Douglas and A.G. Hart of the University of Chicago, and Yale economist Irving Fisher, who recognized that the problem was the fractional reserve system of banking.
- Their advice was not implemented, so the depression only ended when World War II required government to increase its expenditures and to supplement its borrowing from individuals and banks with Fed-created interest-free money.
- Near the war's end the industrial powers reached an agreement at Bretton Woods to stabilize exchange rates at prescribed levels.
- The early post-World War II years represented capitalism's greatest success. Demand management ensured jobs for people who wanted to work. Productivity was high, wage settlements were not unreasonable, and very low real interest rates kept the total debt to GDP ratio more or less constant.
- The Bretton Woods agreement eventually proved to be unworkable and the last vestige of the gold standard had to be abandoned in 1971 when the established parity was wildly out of line with the market price.
- In the latter half of the 1960s, in a worldwide phenomenon, big labor demanded and big business granted wage increases far in excess of productivity increases. Unit labor costs rose, followed by prices.
- The phenomenon put central banks in the invidious position where if they allowed the money supply to expand at a rate that would "clear the market" at the higher price levels, there would be rampant inflation. If they refused, there would be massive unemployment. In the event, most central banks compromised and gave us too much of each at the same time. We called it stagflation.

- A number of incomes policies were invoked in an attempt to control the wage-price spiral. Some worked quite successfully for a while but eventually they all failed. The most common reasons were that they were voluntary, and consequently unworkable in the long run, too bureaucratic, or too unjust in that the benefits of productivity were not fairly distributed.
- In the post-Korean War era, for the first time in the history of the world, nominal wages increased by a multiple of productivity every year for more than 25 consecutive years.
- The consequences of this phenomenon were not immediately recognized by mainline economists. (**understatement**)
- Terms like "natural rate of unemployment" were invented by economists in an effort to explain a development they either didn't understand, or refused to acknowledge.
- Economists, meanwhile, abandoned any serious attempt to understand why incomes policies that had been tried in various countries had ultimately failed and consequently made no serious effort to devise new ones. Instead, they applied abstract mathematical formulae to political economy – a dubious approach at best.
- One mathematical approach (monetarism) maintains that all inflation is caused by increasing the money supply faster than the output of real goods and services and that, by extension, there is no such thing as wage-push inflation.
- The attempt to apply this theory in the real economy produced disastrous results – both social and economic.
- The Western monetary system almost collapsed. A great recession, the worst since the Great Depression, was induced.
- Economies slowed, government revenues fell, deficits increased and these were rolled over into debt which has been compounding at high interest rates ever since.
- Real interest rates rose and became very volatile.

- Communism, or state capitalism, which emerged as the principal alternative to laissez-faire capitalism, foundered because its decision-making apparatus was too centralized. Decisions were too slow and the expertise too limited to be efficient.
- Big deficits and high real interest rates persist in many capitalist countries.
- So does high unemployment and slow growth. The situation is a bit reminiscent of the 1930s.
- Mainline economists and financial papers give governments the same advice that they gave in 1932. Plus ça change, plus c'est la même chose.
- No recognized economic school is even talking about the possibility of achieving full employment and stable prices simultaneously, and the conventional wisdom is so encrusted with its own rhetoric that the idea is met with disbelief.

Even a congenital optimist is likely to be depressed by reading the historical list. It appears that we have learned nothing from the experience of the last 60 years and are resolutely determined to repeat the mistakes that cost us so dearly. Little wonder that despondency is widespread and social unrest is bubbling to the surface.

LAISSEZ-FAIRE: SALVATION OR DAMNATION?

In *Adam Smith's Mistake: How a Moral Philosopher Invented Economics and Ended Morality*, Kenneth Lux argues that the benevolent influence of Smith's "invisible hand" has been inflated beyond all reason by the economics profession. Though it is hailed as a guiding principle, its validity is at least as much myth as reality.

After reviewing the period of British history that followed the publication of Smith's *Wealth of Nations*, Lux observed: "This period saw the establishment of the discipline and tradition of economics. In their attempt to allow the "natural" law of self-interest to operate and to produce its expected beneficent effects, the economists set forth the doctrine of laissez-faire. For them laissez-faire meant opposing any social welfare legislation, such as laws restricting child labor and the length of the working day or laws that regulated working conditions in general."[1]

As in most theories Smith's thesis contains some truth and much nonsense. Consider first Smith's best remembered assertion. "It is not from the benevolence of the butcher, the brewer, or the baker, that we expect our dinner, but from their regard to their own interest."[2] There are innumerable examples of individuals and firms developing products, improving techniques and offering services which, in the pursuit of their own self-interest in the form of sales and profits, have provided the public at large with greater choice, better quality and improved service. At the same time the number of examples of greed, avarice, cutting corners and downright cheating, which have not enhanced the public good, are legion.

It was in the mine-owners self-interest to employ children in their coal mines and it took an act of parliament to end the practice. It was in the self-interest of plantation owners to have slaves and it took a civil war to end the practice. It was in the self-interest of big business to underpay its workers and it took union power to redress the balance. The inevitable exception was Henry Ford who realized that mass production demands mass markets, which means that ordinary workers need sufficient income to buy the goods that they produce.

It is in the self-interest of pimps to let someone else earn an income for them but is it just? It is in the self-interest of drug dealers to get more and more people hooked on drugs but where is the divine interference on behalf of the people whose lives are wrecked by addiction? It is in the self-interest of the banks to operate with insignificant cash reserves to back up their deposits – a practice they can only get away with due to the implied undertaking by the Fed to monetize enough of the government or other debt instruments they hold to provide liquidity in time of crisis. But is it just that the public be required to guarantee their own money in order to subsidize the owners of the banks?

In the decade 1895-1905 it was in the self-interest of the Rockefellers, Mellons, Carnegies and Morgans to gobble up other people's companies and reduce competition in the process. But was it in the public interest to reduce competition to the extent that occurred? Rockefeller's intent, as he often admitted, was to protect himself and his company from "ruinous competition". It is interesting to note that most of the industrial giants insist on competitive prices from their various suppliers while eschewing it for themselves. Pure competition? Not by a country mile. It was an era of amalgamation, trust formation, and power consolidation leading in some cases to monopoly. As J.K. Galbraith points out in *A Journey Through Economic Time*, in the absence of competition, "the whole social justification for the system was, to say the least, at risk. This led inexorably to the further conclusion: if there is monopoly, the state must limit its power – either dissolve or regulate it. The classical system not only allowed state intervention to this end but in a very real sense demanded it."[3]

A hundred years later merger-mania has once again become epidemic. November 1995 news reports suggest that the year will set a new record in what is essentially a repeat of the trend so prevalent at the end of the last century. Competition is being systematically reduced and the new global giants are following the lead set by Rockefeller when he moved his consolidated Standard Oil to New Jersey to save taxes. They are locating their facilities in those jurisdictions with the lowest wages, least taxes, laxest environmental regulations and, in some cases, the highest subsidies.

The consolidation process appears to be in the self-interest of the managers and shareholders but is the public interest equally served? When bank borrowing is involved, the money stock of all citizens is diluted. The interest on the bank financing is deductible from taxable income with its corresponding raid on the treasury. Ordinary taxpayers are given the dubious pleasure of subsidizing the fortunate few. This practice generates far less moral outrage than does comparable subsidies to the poor.

The history of economics since Adam Smith is one that demonstrates beyond doubt that laissez-faire, in the absence of law and regulation, is little more than a license to pilfer and molest. There are many honest business men and women and many altruists. But there are others who push self-interest to the limit and for whom the invisible hand is one with which to surreptitiously pick someone else's pocket.

Common sense demands rules that give effect to common decency. It follows, therefore, that too little regulation is equally unacceptable as too much. The American political system comprises a system of checks and balances and the economic system works best when it is similarly ordered. A rule that is far more appropriate than the mythical invisible hand of Adam Smith, is John Stuart Mills admonition that the rights of an individual or group end at the point where they begin to trespass on the rights of another individual or group. There is no safer foundation for law or regulation.

ECONOMIC FUNDAMENTALISM

The malaise of the mid-1990s is a direct consequence of economic fundamentalism. Like fundamentalists of all stripes, many economists refuse to let facts interfere with their beliefs. They pretend that we have a pure market economy when, in fact, we don't. They treat contemporary inflation as if it were the inflation of the 19th or early 20th centuries when, in fact, there is a world of difference. The consequences of this flight from reality have been social and economic fallout on a scale which should have ended with the Great Depression.

When the Nobel Memorial Prize for Economic Science was established in 1969, Professor Erik Lundberg observed that "economic science has developed increasingly in the direction of a mathematical specification and statistical quantification of economic contexts." Its "techniques of mathematical and statistical analysis", Lundberg explained, have "proven successful" and have left far behind "the vague, more literary type of economics" with which most laymen may be familiar.[4] Lundberg was correct in his observation that economic science has become increasingly obsessed with mathematical formulae. But that has been its undoing. The attempt to equate the discipline of political economy, which is a unique mixture of art and science, with pure sciences like physics and chemistry has removed it further and further from reality.

No school of economics bears a greater responsibility for this aberration than the current Chicago School. The high incidence of Nobel laureates amongst its scholars is consistent with Lundberg's perception of the evolution of economics. A more jaundiced observer might detect a certain irony in rewarding a school of thought primarily responsible for the theory which has done more damage to the real economy than any theory since Jean Baptiste Say first proclaimed his infamous diversion from reality.

The greatest losers in both cases have been the legions of men and women who have been barred from gainful employment. A job equates with human dignity. The right to gainful employment is just as fundamental as freedom of speech and religion. In our complex societies a job is living expression of self-worth. So it is a genuine tragedy to see the Fed, backed and encouraged by the economic fundamentalists, determined to prevent unemployment from falling much below 6 percent and thereby condemning innocent men and women to involuntary idleness. At what point does the apathy and indifference of a fundamentalist "right" become a human wrong?

Unquestionably one of the most disappointing and disillusioning consequences of the monetarist counter-revolution has been an unacceptably high level of unemployment. This has always bothered me and fresh salt was poured in the old wound early on the morning of May 19, 1994, as I listened to a radio report of a question and answer period with Milton Friedman following his address at Vancouver's Fraser Institute the previous day. Question to Dr. Friedman:

"If you had been invited to the G-7 meeting on unemployment, what advice would you have provided to the ministers? Answer:

"I wouldn't have attended, ha, ha, but the answer is quite simple. The problem that they were dealing with is unemployment, is a government-created problem, created by excessive regulation of the terms and conditions under which people can be employed. If you make it very expensive for people to employ people, they're going to employ fewer than if you don't, and what's happened in many of the Western countries, including to a lesser extent the United States, is that the gap between the cost to the employer of hiring a person and the return to the employee from being hired, that gap has widened, and in some of the European countries it's 50%. If you take a place like France, where they have very high social security – so-called social security taxes – and the way to eliminate the unemployment is to open up the market, to free the markets, to let wages be determined by the market and to eliminate all of the extra costs that are piled on by extra regulation. It's hard to fire people. If it's hard to fire people, people will be very careful about hiring them, so I don't think that's a very complicated problem. What's complicated is the political [will]. Like so many of these [problems], it's easy to say what you should do, but it's very hard to do it, because of the political vested interests that are involved."[5]

As I listened intently I thought to myself "This is a cop-out. This is the kind of answer politicians give to a question when they don't know the answer." I suspect that is the truth, and that monetarists really do not know how to square the human tragedy of involuntary idleness with the neat precision of their mathematical imperative.

Of course government regulations are an impediment to enterprise and certainly there are persons on Unemployment Insurance or welfare who are better off than they would be working at a minimum wage. But these conditions, which must be addressed if the system is ever to achieve its highest level of performance possible, do not come within a country mile of explaining the Organization for Economic Co-operation and Development's projection of 35 million unemployed in 1995.[6] Ninety percent of the problem is the same one that has plagued Western economies periodically for two hundred years, i.e. a shortage of aggregate demand, even if the reasons for it have changed.

How, then, can full employment – defined as a rough equilibrium between job seekers and job openings – be achieved? By declaring war? Curiously, I have never talked to anyone, even the most conservative economist, who didn't agree that if the United States declared war tomorrow, and it turned out to be a protracted war, that full employment would be achieved within two years. One minute they are insisting that programs be cut and budgets balanced and a minute later, when cornered, they agree that in the event of war none of that would matter.

Hasn't it ever struck you as peculiar that our best and brightest are quite capable of that kind of hat-trick in time of war, in order to produce a whole list of items that are of no earthly use except for killing, while they appear to be quite incapable of comparable ingenuity in winning the peace? It's time for another war, but not one of bombs and guns. It's time that we waged war against pollution, inadequate housing, illiteracy, sickness, poverty and hunger, decaying infrastructure, urban blight and, above all, indifference. Engaging in all these wars will be more than enough to achieve full employment; and it can be done without the inflation associated with a shooting war.

CHAPTER 12

THE PACKAGE OF
ECONOMIC REFORMS

*"I repeat ... that all power is a trust - that we are
accountable for its exercise - that, from the people,
and for the people, all springs and all must exist. "*

Benjamin Disraeli

MONETARY REFORM

The most far-reaching of the proposed reforms is, of
course, monetary reform. The way money is created must be
changed so there is less reliance on debt. How many times in
the course of a week do you read or hear the word debt used?
Often? Yet how can it be otherwise when for 200 years nearly
all the new money created has been created as debt on which
interest has to be paid and no one has created the money with
which to pay the interest on that ever-increasing mountain of
debt.

The objects and benefits of moving gently but firmly
away from near-total reliance on a fractional reserve banking
system are many and profound. It will be easier for federal
governments to achieve and maintain balanced budgets and,
with the increased facility available to them, to share burdens
with other levels of government so that state and city governments, too, will be able to balance revenue and income. In

addition, the change will, over time, substantially increase bank reserves. This will make them less vulnerable to "runs" and failures from any cause. It will make the world system less volatile and subject to collapse. An extra dividend is that the public's contingent liability for deposit insurance will be substantially reduced.

The importance of giving governments greater latitude in balancing their budgets, without the necessity of raising the entire sum by means of higher explicit taxes, is a function of changes in life style and priority. As we have moved from a family-oriented, agriculture-dominated to a more industrialized, impersonal society, many of the functions formerly financed by the family must now be financed by the state. In a predominantly agricultural America families cared for the sick and the elderly at home. While there is much nostalgia for that system it is not possible, in the majority of circumstances, to turn the clock back. This is especially so in families that require two incomes in order to pay for the basic necessities.

In addition, industrialization creates new and increased responsibility for the state. Private enterprise invents, develops, manufactures and profits from the sale of automobiles. The state is then obliged to build and maintain roads and bridges. Private enterprise invents, develops, manufactures and profits from the sale of airplanes. The state is required to build and maintain airports and provide customs and immigration services as people in larger numbers travel out of country. The list could go on and on but the bottom line is that governments spend a much larger share of total national income than they did until recent decades and if the whole is raised by explicit taxes the level of taxation becomes a disincentive to earn taxable income.

AN INCOMES POLICY

This is absolutely essential to maximize the benefit from monetary reform. If the new money created each year is distributed vertically, through higher wages for the already employed and consequently higher prices for existing output, it will not be available to finance additional employment and increased output. If there is any one concept which must be learned in order to understand the failure of monetarism it is this. To the extent that the increase in money stock – translated into income – is distributed vertically, in excess of increases in productivity, it contributes to higher wages and prices rather than increased output. Unless wage increases to the already employed are limited to the average increase in real output, inflation will continue and if inflation continues interest rates will be higher than necessary because lenders will continue to demand a premium as a hedge against the anticipated inflation. This has negative implications for governments and for the economy as a whole. It is the people who must bear the extra burden.

The other great advantage of continuous low inflation is that it permits a significantly higher level of employment. If there is one benefit which tops the list from a humanitarian point of view it is the availability of jobs for people who want to work. This has been the over-riding motive in my life-long obsession with economics because I think the need to contribute to the common well-being is fundamental to one's feeling of self worth. Finally, it should be noted, negligible inflation protects the value of savings for everyone.

TIGHTER BANKING REGULATIONS

The thought of regulations gives bankers nightmares. The only regulations they really like are the ones they promote themselves like reducing reserve requirements from the original 50% at the time the Bank of England was first chartered to as low as 3% or even 0% for certain kinds of deposits today. If they are to continue to have any special privilege to "print" money, even if it is only to half the extent that they currently enjoy, banks will have to review and rework the whole concept of the "public trust" that this implies.

Nothing irritates me quite as fast as a bank spokesperson saying, in response to the suggestion that they make more money available to small business, "We have to act as guardians of our depositors' money." Such fatuous double-speak! What they are really saying is that "we, and we alone, will decide for whom we will create loans and we prefer governments, brokers and big business because that way we can make more money for less work." If they were only concerned about the safety of existing deposits they would have been less cavalier in making loans to Third World governments, large real-estate developers and the leveraged-buyout monopoly players. It was the banks' greed, rather than their prudence as guardians of their depositors' money, which ruled the day.

If the whole idea of creating new money is to facilitate the creation of new wealth in the form of increased output, then the entire addition to the money stock should be directed to that purpose. In effect, new loans should be made for either investment or consumption because they are the two sides of the same coin! I cannot remember a market for anything that some enterprising entrepreneur didn't try to capitalize on. But if, as in the Great Depression, and in one or two recent recessions, existing capacity exceeds demand, entrepreneurs are unlikely to line up for loans to create additional redundant capacity. So consumption, which creates income and savings for others, and investment are Siamese twins which cannot be separated.

It is the small businesses which create the most jobs and increased output that have the most difficulty getting bank financing. In the Spring of 1994, Helen Sinclair, president of the Canadian Bankers Association, cited one of the best known excuses. She admitted that banks have a problem in their relationship with small business but defended their caution by pointing out that federal government statistics show 50 percent of all small businesses don't make it past their fifth birthday.[1] That may be so but an equally interesting and important statistic would be the percentage which failed because their bank took away the safety net just as they jumped from the high wire. I have never known an entrepreneur, myself included, whose bank didn't try to put them out of business at one stage or another of their development. So perhaps it would be in the country's interest if a certain proportion of new loans had to be made to small business with limited or no collateral where the investors, as a condition, were willing to risk their own savings. Character assessment might be part of the consideration. It is one which appears to have been pretty well disregarded in recent decades. With these conditions satisfied, the banks should be prepared to lose and write off some proportion of the small loans each year. It should satisfy their irresistible urge to gamble if they were to gamble on people who want to build real products and provide real services for a change.

This brings me to what banks should increasingly not be allowed to do. They should not be allowed to create money to make loans to foreign governments. Instead they might pool a little money and provide microbanking facilities to the world's potential entrepreneurs capable of providing employment and income to the teeming millions struggling to escape their poverty. It probably won't win me any marks to quote Chairman Mao but he spoke wisely when he said "Give a man a fish and you feed him for a day; teach a man to fish and you feed him for a lifetime." If the American dream means anything, it is a sign of wisdom to extend that dream to the widest extent possible both at home and worldwide.

One other banking practice that should be phased out as rapidly as possible is making loans for the purchase of stocks and bonds on margin. Buying stocks on margin is a classic example of spreading new money vertically to increase the price of the stocks without increasing the underlying real value of the assets. It is classic inflation. If stock ownership is supposed to represent savings, let it represent real savings instead of leverage.

Nowhere is the prohibition more urgent than in respect to companies buying shares in other companies with borrowed money and then deducting the interest from income for tax purposes. This particular raid on the treasury is as direct and rewarding as an armed hold-up. The only difference is that one is legal and the other is not. It is a practice, however, which should be ended because it creates no new wealth and adds to the concentration of existing wealth at taxpayers' expense. The chief financial officer of a large Canadian conglomerate once said that it was his job to see that no one company under his umbrella paid tax in any one year. The high leverage operation he was associated with did suffer some pain when the 1990-91 recession struck but meanwhile the government-facilitated transfer of wealth from the poor and average income taxpayers to the rich owners of the conglomerate was staggering.

There are two important exceptions to this rule that I would recommend to policy makers reflecting on the question. The first would be some figure – say $50,000 – as a one-time credit for the purchase of common shares. The purpose is two-fold. Although the number of applicants might not be great at first, use of the facility would extend the benefits of capitalism to a greater number of people and at the same time would allow employees to purchase shares in their company and participate as owners as well as workers. Employee Stock Ownership Plans (ESOPs) have been shown to be beneficial in that they produce a happier and consequently more productive work force. A Toronto Stock Exchange fact sheet reported: "Quantitative analysis also indicates that ESOP companies are dramatically outperforming their competitors in terms of profit-ability, return on equity, and return on capital. Further, these companies exhibit significantly lower debt-equity levels compared to other TSE-listed firms in their sectors."[2] The maximum figure chosen for the plan would have to be deter-mined fiscally, that is how much income tax revenue could government afford to give up as a result of permitting the deduction of interest on the bank loans.

The second exception would be a much larger exemption for entrepreneurs buying shares in their own company in which they are engaged full time. This carrot would be a combination incentive and reward for the creation of new jobs and new wealth. It is an aspect of the American dream which should be encouraged. At the same time it is not a benefit which should apply equally to managers and officers of widely held companies. They have shown an amazing ingenuity in looking after their own interests so any stock they buy, in excess of the rule for all citizens, should be from after tax dollars, that is, real savings.

Speculation in bonds and derivatives is even more worrisome. A 1994 article in the *New Federalist* sounded a warning bell.

"Since the beginning of February, significantly more than $1 trillion worth of so-called 'financial assets' has been wiped out, in panic selling of leveraged positions built up using derivative instruments over the past five years of Federal Reserve-engineered declining interest rates. Down the tubes have gone the now-notorious 'hedge funds,' set up to circumvent the provisions of the Investment Company Act of 1940, and deploying an estimated 15-fold leverage on assets or collateral of up to $100 billion. Gone is J.P. Morgan's market in so-called 'emerging market debt.' Going, the so-called 'collateralized mortgage obligations' and their principal and interest 'strips'; going, the municipal bonds, as 'lenders' who have financed leveraged positions sell off the collateral in what is being described as 'a kind of global margin call.'

"And it's only the beginning. The trillion dollars-plus that evaporated over the last two months is embedded in the $12-16 trillion total notional value of global derivative instruments traded. That comes next.

"For example, U.S. banks have lent some 3.7% of their assets to finance margin purchases of bonds and other securities by borrowers like 'hedge funds.' That is more than $700 billion of such loans. And it is also some 2.5 times the paid-in capital of the banks. It doesn't include banks' purchases of securities for their own accounts. What they have lent has been put into hock by the borrowers to build up their leverage. Keeping such an inverted pyramid balanced on its apex is what the derivatives managers call 'risk management.'"[3]

Breaking the wild horses on this one will not be easy. Two approaches have been suggested. The first is to subject banks to fairly strict regulations as to the derivatives they can write. Congressman Henry B. Gonzalez, former Chairman of the House Committee on Banking Reform and Urban Affairs has been leading the way on this front. The alternative is to impose a 0.1% tax on them as proposed by Lyndon LaRouche. In a March 28, 1993, press conference, Representative Gonzalez told those who were listening that adoption of such a tax would bring what has developed to a halt "overnight."[4]

There are several reasons why effective action of some kind is urgently required. The first, and probably most important, is to wean bankers away from the gambling mentality in favor of a development mentality. This is a big switch which will not happen easily or overnight. The second reason is that derivatives can be a major source of world financial market instability. No one I have talked to could say precisely the extent of the instability but the opinions ranged from significant to potentially critical. A combination of billions of exposure in derivatives, in the same wolf pack as other billions of hot money chasing around the world in search of speculative "opportunities", is enough to destabilize any system and render it vulnerable to collapse. It is a risk that can be avoided. Finally there is the question of reporting and of keeping shareholders fully informed as to how many of their chips are riding on what numbers. These are all good reasons to apply a harness.

If the banks do not want to operate in a way that treats money-creation as a public trust then the only alternative would be for governments to create all the new money, allow banks to lend only the real money depositors chose to entrust to them, and let them charge the full cost of the banking services they provide to those persons willing to pay. Personally I prefer the 50% solution proposed earlier because it is both politically and operationally more acceptable. But only if the banks are willing to accept a more responsible role.

THE EFFECT ON BANKS

The immediate effect on the banking industry would be minimal, except they would have to curtail new loans, and be more selective in the ones they make. They would still have their revenue producing assets but total assets would not increase nearly as fast as they have in the past. Consequently the rate of increase in future profitability could be affected.

The overall effect will be mitigated and probably lost in the context of the banking revolution which is already underway. Chemical Bank is merging with Chase Manhattan.[5]

Bank of Boston Wins Bid to Buy Boston Bancorp in a Stock Swap.[6] Lloyds Bank Agrees To Merge With TSB Group P.L.C. a rival bank.[7] In what appears to be a worldwide phenomenon one reads of bank mergers or rumours of bank mergers almost weekly. The repercussions are already far-reaching and include the elimination of branches and the elimination of people as Automated Teller Machines and electronic banking encroach inexorably on the provision of line services. One article captioned "Teller, Beware" estimated that the Chase Chemical merger will cost 12,000 jobs.[8] Another, from Frankfurt, said "Deutsche Bank Plan To Cut 10,000 Jobs"[9]

The extent of the revolution in banking techniques is impossible to gauge at this point but there is little doubt that revolution is the right word. An article in the *Wall Street Journal* was headed "On-Line Banking Has Bankers Fretting PCs May Replace Branches[10] At about the same time Braxton Associates, the financial services consulting arm of Deloitte & Touche, estimated that the spread of electronic and telephone banking and other technological change will slash about half the branches and almost one-quarter of the employees from Canada's retail banking system over the next decade.[11] It appears that the banking industry will be constantly adjusting for a decade at least so I can think of no better time to reduce their reliance on government largesse. I, for one, have little doubt that bankers have the resilience to make the necessary adjustments and still land firmly on their feet.

A TAX ON FOREIGN EXCHANGE TRANSACTIONS

There is no part of the financial economy in greater need of being slowed down than the currency traders. Clipping the wings of these high-flyers is the fourth essential economic reform. It has been estimated that the volume of currency transactions now exceeds $1 trillion a day – a sum so large that it is greater than the annual gross domestic product of many countries. Exchange transactions on that scale accomplish no earthly good. Most of it is speculation, pure and simple, and totally disruptive of the domestic economies which become its targets of convenience.

Reformers were hoping that the leaders of the G-7 group of nations would take advantage of their meeting in Halifax, in the summer of 1995, to recommend the universal imposition of a tax along the lines of the one first proposed by Nobel Prize-winning U.S. economist James Tobin, in 1978.[12] The rate proposed was 0.5 percent and it has been estimated that if the tax were imposed on a global basis it could increase government revenues by $300 to $400 billion per annum.[13]

Unfortunately, the leaders of the industrial world blew their golden opportunity. Their cool response was stated in the G-7 communiqué as follows: "Internal and external balances, together with unhelpful fluctuations in financial and currency markets, could jeopardize achievement of sustained non-inflationary growth as well as the continued expansion of international trade."[14]

The world leaders' detachment from reality can be understood, thought not necessarily condoned, by anyone familiar with the fact that they don't write their own communiqués. This one, obviously, was written by economic fundamentalists who fail to comprehend that unbridled self-interest has no saving grace. It is simply savagery – the law of the jungle. There is no invisible hand guiding currency traders except the one they slip into the pockets of taxpayers worldwide.

Instead of adopting a contemporary solution, the G-7 leaders opted for more of the same – an improved early warning system, and the establishment of a new "Emergency Financing Mechanism" to speed up access to the IMF by countries with weak currencies. So one more time ordinary people will be taxed for the benefit of financiers and speculators at the additional cost of jobs and opportunities for themselves.

Anyone naive enough to think that the IMF, working with central banks, can do the job of stabilizing currencies that are either over-valued or under-valued should read *The Vandals' Crown: How Rebel Currency Traders Overthrew the World's Central Banks*, by Gregory J. Millman.[15] In it Millman gives chapter and verse of the evolution of financial markets and the development of techniques, including options, that challenge the authority and independence of central banks and national governments alike. The same story emerges in *The Confidence Game*. In a few cases concerted efforts by central bankers in several countries has made a difference but, more often, it has not. And almost always it is the taxpayers who have been ripped off when the dust of battle clears. Democracy is at stake.

I hear and read so much news that annoys me that I have become more or less immune; but when a question of great principle is discussed my ears open. One such occasion was a Sunday morning broadcast, September 24, 1995, of the Canadian Broadcasting Corporation, on the subject of economics. The person being interviewed was Mansoor Ijaz, an American ex-nuclear physicist who now runs an investment firm in New York – a place he finds too dangerous to raise his family – so he and his family live in a three-storey open concept home complete with a tennis court and a swimming pool just north of Toronto. Ijaz believes economic forecasts are an anachronism because people like him run our economies now. Ijaz gave the interviewer his view of how the world economy works.

"By-and-large central bankers in the world, as well as politicians that make economic decisions, are totally irrelevant to the process. Hedge-funds, speculators, with the information age, with the globalization of the economy, with the money managers being able to move money just at a drop of a hat, all kinds of changes in the way the world that we live in have taken place – what they [central bankers and politicians] say anymore is irrelevant because there is no central bank in the world that can take on the top three or four speculators in the world, any day of the week, there is just no way that they can do it. They just don't have enough money. The fact of the matter is that guys like us don't rip economies apart. In those places where we see that politicians are doing things that are inappropriate we hold their feet to the fire. And the way in which we do that is to move money from point A to point B and that will not change ever again in the history of the world. I think, in fact, we are more like a supra-national government of the world."[16]

The unmitigated arrogance! Currency traders not only run the world but by some divine right, conferred by the invisible hand of self-interest, they are entitled to run the world. Both politicians and central banks are totally irrelevant to the process? That is increasingly the case but it is preposterous that it should be so. Stopping the overnight currency traders in their tracks would be a good place to start. They perceive themselves as international policemen holding politicians feet to the fire when in fact they are international vampires sucking the life-blood from one economy after another.

A good starting point in the re-imposition of checks and balances would be a tax of 0.5 percent on all exchange transactions. No one can estimate precisely how much the tax would yield because the volume of transactions would diminish very rapidly. But it would be enough, together with the other measures proposed in this book, to put the U.S. federal budget in surplus in less than two years.

There is no reason why national governments, rather than the United Nations as some people have proposed, should not be the beneficiaries of the tax. Certainly that kind of windfall would make it a lot easier for national governments, including the United States, to keep current with their UN contributions.

One of the objections to the so-called "Tobin tax" is the suggestion that it couldn't be collected. I don't believe it. All of my adult life I have been dealing with bureaucrats who insisted that something couldn't be done and then, when they were told to do it, miraculously discovered that it was possible after all. I could write a whole book on this subject but two brief examples are illustrative.

For many years members of the Canadian Armed Forces were embarrassed because their votes in general elections were counted and made public a week to ten days after voting day and sometimes the pattern of their votes was quite different from the public at large. In close elections the results in several constituencies (districts) might be uncertain until the service vote was known.

Repeated requests to the Chief Electoral Officer that some means be found to solve the problem, over a period of many years, always evoked the same answer. It can't be done. Finally, in total exasperation, the Chief Electoral Officer was directed by the responsible politicians to find a solution. He found, to everyone's delight, that service men and women could vote in advance and have their votes counted and reported simultaneously with the rest of the population in a way that attracted no special attention. Problem solved.

In another case it was the long-held view of numerous observers that it would be fun to turn the Rideau canal, situated just below the parliament buildings in Ottawa, into a skating rink in winter. Several voluminous official reports concluded that it couldn't be done. Eventually the chairman of the National Capital Commission, under whose jurisdiction it was, decided it would be done anyway. It was, and for many years now has been the world's longest skating rink enjoyed by hundreds of thousands of skaters including numerous U.S. visitors to Canada's capital city.

The examples are legion but the conclusion is this – a hefty tax to slow down speculative currency trading and encourage money managers to consider longer-term investment as an alternative to short-term speculation is not only possible, it is absolutely essential to the well-being of national economies individually and the world economy of which they are a part.

CENTRAL BANK ACCOUNTABILITY

People who are concerned about inflation and nothing else may be seduced into believing that central bank autonomy is central to their view of the future. Why this is so is a bit difficult to explain when, as Paul Volcker points out in his Foreword to *The Central Banks*: "It is a sobering fact that the prominence of central banks in this century has coincided with a general tendency towards more inflation, not less."[17]

Both the authors of *The Central Banks*, Marjorie Deane and Robert Pringle, and Steven Solomon, author of *The Confidence Game*, came to the conclusion that central banks should be autonomous, though Solomon did so with grave misgivings. I am obliged to disagree to the depths of my being, based on both principle and performance. Let me begin with performance.

People who give central banks credit for bringing the double-digit inflation of the 1970s under significant control have not included on their balance sheets the debits for the damage that has been created in the process. Millions of people lost their jobs thanks to central banks. Thousands of farmers lost their farms, often after several generations in the family, thanks to central banks. Tens of thousands of people lost their homes as a result of the high mortgage interest rates imposed by central banks. Untold thousands of businesses have been bankrupted thanks to central banks and an army of men and women have given up hope for the future as a result of central bank policies.

If all that carnage isn't sufficient to indict them, consider the massive transfer of wealth from poor to rich as a result of interest-rate policy. In addition, the Western world has seen its debt load skyrocket to the point where an economic meltdown is inevitable in the absence of radical reform. The U.S. government is $2-$2.5 trillion deeper in debt thanks to "practical monetarism" as inflicted on an unsuspecting public by the Fed.

AND THE PROBLEM IS FAR FROM UNDER CONTROL

While both the Fed and the Bank of Canada rate an overall grade of D or F – depending on the severity of the grading – on overall performance for the last 15 years, and consequently strike out on performance alone, it is even more difficult to forgive what they have done to the political process. They have undermined public confidence in politicians and political institutions to an alarming extent. Politicians promise jobs and opportunity and central banks make it impossible for them to deliver.

Paul Volcker disregarded the concerns of the Carter administration when he first raised interest rates dramatically yet it was Jimmy Carter who was to reap the whirlwind and economic policy is acknowledged to have been a factor in his defeat in the presidential election of 1980. In the area of public life which affects electors most directly – in their pocketbooks – the Chairman of the Fed is more powerful than the President of the United States. Similarly the Governor of the Bank of Canada, which has chosen to pursue monetarism like a monkey on the Fed's back, is more powerful than the Prime Minister of Canada. This development is a perversion of democracy and is wrong! wrong! wrong! What is the point of putting politicians and people through the gut-wrenching exercise of periodic elections when the alleged winners will be powerless to act creatively when elected; destructively, maybe, but not creatively.

This usurpation of power is the greater sin in the United States where the Fed is privately owned and can be assumed to be acting, consciously or subconsciously, in the best interests of its owners and this may or may not be equally in the public interest. To the extent that the Fed exercises near total control over the money supply and short-term interest rates and, as a consequence, control over the growth rate of the economy and the level of unemployment, it cannot be said that the U.S. enjoys government of, by and for the people. Instead it is government of the banks, by the banks, and for the banks with public benefits that can be characterized as crumbs from the King's table. The pursuit of economic efficiency suggests that central banks be ultimately responsible to their national governments and democratic principles demand that they be accountable.

ABOLISH THE INTERNATIONAL MONETARY FUND?

Having discussed the five essential reforms for a sane and enduring capitalist system I turn now to some ideas that are not essential but nevertheless worth looking at. The first of these is the possible winding-up of the IMF since it is now an anachronism.

The IMF was a child of the Bretton Woods System which pegged the U.S. dollar to gold and other currencies to the dollar. Its purpose was to support the currency system and to aid nations experiencing painful real economic adjustments. These included real economic changes such as rising unemployment, lower domestic prices and increases in excess capacity as an alternative to changes in the exchange rate.

The whole notion of fixed exchange rates proved to be an economic albatross. In essence it meant that domestic economies should be run in the interests of exchange rate parity rather than in the interests of citizen taxpayers. It was an idea deeply embedded in the gold standard and the deification of money. But it didn't make sense, and the whole system broke down as was inevitable.

It is a mark of the intellectual bankruptcy of the economic fundamentalists that they are suggesting a return to a new Bretton Woods with currencies pegged to a narrow band of exchange relative to key currencies. They cite as their reason the increased volatility of currencies in the years since the Bretton Woods system collapsed. There was less volatility in the years when the system was first in place so, by extension, there would be less volatility again if a similar system was agreed.

The inference results entirely from a misreading of economic history. The stability occurred at a time when most industrial economies had common characteristics. They enjoyed low and relatively consistent interest rates, high growth rates, high levels of employment and wage settlements not too far above productivity rates, and consequently relatively little inflation. Real relative values of currencies changed slowly and consequently there was little pressure on exchange rates.

Then everything began to change. Wage increases ceased to bear any relationship to productivity; rates of settlements varied widely between countries; so did inflation rates and consequently the real relative values of currencies; the introduction of the monetarist counter-revolution led to a system where interest rates go up and down like a roller coaster with international capital in hot pursuit of the highest rates.

Exchange rate volatility increased dramatically and it will remain as long as these conditions exist or if they recur. No amount of support from central banks and no amount of meddling by the IMF can guarantee exchange rate stability in the face of rapidly changing relative values.

If it is important to have greater stability in exchange rates this can be achieved by creating a climate of stability, that is, wage increases compatible with productivity increases, low inflation, low and consistent interest rates, high employment and consistent growth rates. If the economies of the major trading nations were all stable, exchange rates would be reasonably stable and change slowly – a condition which no amount of tinkering could achieve as long as economies operate as they currently do.

Meanwhile the IMF has lost its raison d'être and is searching for a new one. Of its several avenues of exploration the thing it is best at is meddling in other people's business. It is always telling countries how to run their economies and it is usually in the American way even if that is totally inappropriate to the best interests of the country in question.

A case in point is its recent advice to Canada. In October, 1995, the IMF said in its world economic outlook report: "The credibility of the government's economic policies would be strengthened by the adoption of stronger medium-term consolidation programs aimed at bringing the federal fiscal deficit well below the present target of 3% of G.D.P." At the same time it slashed Canada's growth-rate projection to 2.2%, for 1995, down from its forecast in May of 4.3%. I wonder why they thought the economy had slowed so dramatically? Was the dismissal of thousands of public servants a factor in the equation, along with the psychological effect of the slash and burn approach to deficit cutting which scares the be-jeepers out of the rest of the population and convinces them not to spend their money?

About that same time the IMF set the Canadian NAIRU at 8.75 percent. I am sure that if you asked IMF managing director Michel Camdessus if Canada should continue its cost-cutting plans until the federal government budget is balanced he would answer "yes, by all means." Yet, in saying so, he might be unaware that since World War II, at least, Canada's federal government has never balanced its budget with more than 7 percent unemployed. So on the one hand the IMF is suggesting to the Bank of Canada that it should not let unemployment fall below 8.75 percent, for fear of losing face with the economic fundamentalists, while at the same time urging a balanced budget which would appear to be impossible with such a high level of unemployment. I cannot say how deeply I resent my money being given to an international agency which gives my government bad advice. It gets a surfeit of that from its own officials.

The other niche that the IMF is filling is providing funds to Third World countries to help them repay international financiers who have made bad loans. That is the essence of its role as set out clearly in *The Confidence Game*. Financiers who are supposed to be the brightest and most knowledgeable of investors make billions in questionable loans to Third World countries. High interest rates induced by the Fed and its accomplices make repayment of the loans, with interest, beyond the capacity of the borrowers. Central banks of the creditor nations can't come directly to the aid of the irresponsible lenders so they persuade the IMF to come to the rescue. The IMF lends the debtor nations money to service the loans on the condition that those countries operate their economies not in the best interests of the health, education and welfare of their citizens, but in a manner best suited to earning the foreign exchange necessary to repay the private loans as well as, in due course, the help from the IMF. This interpretation of IMF policy is mine, of course, but it is not unique.

The financiers who claim to be such all-seeing, all-knowing international policemen should be the first to accept the consequences of their imprudence. If Adam Smith's invisible hand gets lost once in a while so should the money that was directed by its pursuit of self-interest. Certainly the taxpayers of the world should not be expected to rescue financiers from the consequences of their own mismanagement. Yet this is the role assigned to the IMF by world leaders advised by economic fundamentalists whose left invisible hand doesn't appreciate what its right invisible hand is doing.

So, instead of passing the international hat for the IMF one more time, it would be wise to wind it up. It is an organization without a function – at least without a function that could be proven to be legitimate. Its assets could be turned over to the International Development Association, the World Bank's agency that helps poor countries, to assist those Third World countries which have been impoverished by IMF policies.

THE WORLD DOLLAR

I have often wondered if the time hasn't come when it would be desirable to replace the U.S. dollar with a World dollar as the medium of international exchange. At one time the function was performed by gold, though this played havoc with the rate of expansion or contraction of domestic currencies which were tied to the level of gold reserves. With the abandonment of the gold standard the void was filled by the British pound and the U.S. dollar. Over time the burden fell increasingly on the U.S. dollar until recent years when there has been increasing reliance on the German mark and the Japanese yen. In theory there is no particular reason why the burden of international exchange transactions should fall on any particular national currency or currencies. On the contrary, these should be free to fall or rise in relation to a world standard as a measure of their relative performance against the world norm. Indeed that is what exchange rates, which represent a composite price of goods, services and capital goods, are for. Each currency must be allowed to float freely up or down in order to redress the balance of national payments with the world.

When considering the institutional framework for such a development it would appear that of the three existing institutions – the International Monetary Fund, the World Bank, and the Bank for International Settlements (BIS) – there is a need for only two.

The function of one of these would be comparable to the one currently filled by the World Bank and its International

Development Association, albeit with the change in emphasis which is slowly taking place. In addition to its long-standing role of providing funds for infrastructure megaprojects, some of which have been the subject of considerable controversy, the World Bank is increasing its funding of health, welfare, and environmental concerns. An additional dimension of a new vision would be the provision of additional billions for micro-banking which is one of the world's emerging success stories in helping the poorest of the poor to escape their poverty.

The other institutional requirement is a strictly banking function. Presumably it could be performed by a re-organized Bank for International Settlements, although one should be quite skeptical of the credentials of that secretive organization. If a new bank were established to fill the function, the BIS, as well as the IMF, would become redundant.

The international bank, whatever it is called, would obtain its capital from member countries partly as equity and partly in the form of debt instruments that would provide it with income. The international exchange bank would then issue (a) currency for use by world travellers and (b) interest-bearing securities to the extent desired by individual central banks. It would also act as the bank for international settlements as well as arranging swaps between currencies, or between currencies and gold at market prices, in order to facilitate trade as it evolves on a global scale.

It should be possible for central banks to get by with a reduced level of reserves if they stop trying to defend the indefensible at taxpayers expense. To the extent that reserves are required, central banks may desire a mix of national currencies, world currency and gold. It will always be a matter of judgment; and, as experience has shown, preferences change over time. A new world currency would have to earn its spurs but, in time, it would be accepted as the universal international standard against which all national currencies were measured.

TAXATION POLICY

Another area of at least academic interest is taxation

policy. I know it is trendy and politically popular to have a graduated income tax system under which the rich pay higher marginal rates than the poor. I also realize that most of the rich and well-to-do people I know spend countless hours trying to determine how the high rates can be legitimately avoided. Their success, including helpful legislative changes, has been noteworthy.

I have often wondered if a flat-tax system couldn't be devised which would raise just as much income while, at the same time, providing both an incentive to work hard and to pay tax. For discussion purposes it would be interesting to consider a flat-tax of, say, 20% on every dollar of income, including capital gains, over and above a standard non-taxable amount. Allow deductions of 50 percent of gifts to charities and political parties, etc. up to the point where the rate was reduced to 15%, which would be the flat-tax minimum. I don't know how practical it would be but I am sure there is a system which would involve less income juggling and far fewer hours of accountants, and tax consultants, time.

Two other areas of interest are potential gold mines for government. The first is what Canadians call "sin taxes", i.e. taxes on cigarettes, beverage alcohol and gasoline. A case can be made that higher taxes in each of these categories would be in the enlightened "self-interest" of present and future generations. An equally good argument is that it's an easy way to raise money. At this point the Canadian "self-interest" should be publicly stated. Our "sin taxes" are much higher than those in the United States. This leads to much smuggling of these items into Canada as well as a culture shock for American tourists heading north and facing such a big differential between Canadian and U.S. prices for cigarettes, liquor and gasoline. Even a modest closing of the gap would reduce smuggling and mitigate the culture shock.

The second area of tax potential represents the biggest untapped source in existence. I speak of financial transaction taxes. As previously indicated, a tax on exchange transactions alone would provide the treasury with more money than the combined total of all the budget cuts currently being debated by the Congress. But there is no reason why a tax could not also be applied to the purchase and sale of other financial instruments including stocks and bonds. The rationale is the same. Even a small tax would slow down the financial economy, discourage short-term speculation and allow the financial community the privilege of a fairer contribution to the total tax burden. Three good reasons.

MINIMUM WAGES

Few subjects are as controversial as to whether or not minimum wages are a good thing or a bad thing. As Linda Gorman points out in her essay on the subject in the *Encyclopedia of Economics*, "the minimum wage has had widespread political support enjoyed by few other public policies."[18] She is quick to add, however, that "According to a 1978 article in *American Economic Review*, the American Economic Association's main journal, fully 90 percent of the economists surveyed agreed that the minimum wage increases unemployment among low-skilled workers. It also reduces the on-the-job training offered by employers and shrinks the number of positions offering fringe benefits. To those who lose their jobs, their training opportunities, or their fringe benefits as a result of the minimum wage, the law is simply one more example of good intentions producing hellish results.[19]

While I am well aware of these arguments, and of the potential consequences of minimum wages, I find a certain illogic in the objections. Economists say that minimum wages interfere with how wages are determined in a free market. But the market for labor is not free and the illogic arises in having a genuine market at the bottom end of the scale, for the poor, and a "wage leadership" driven monopoly at the top end. The result has been an increasing disparity between classes of workers. Figure 17 is indicative of the trend. The minimum wage was 46% of the average wage in manufacturing in 1959, and only 36% of that same index in 1993.

People working at or near minimum wages, who cannot afford to have faulty wiring or plumbing fixed or leaky roofs repaired, will be even worse off in the years ahead unless the trend is reversed. Either an incomes policy must narrow the gap between workers at the bottom of the heap and their more fortunate brothers and sisters, or else society must accept the consequences of a class system in which the majority earn more than enough to pay their own way, while the minority, comprising the "working poor", never will.

U.S. Wage Differentials (1959-1993)

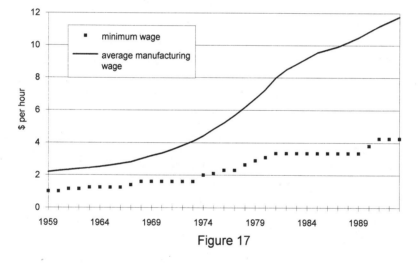

Figure 17

Source: *Economic Report of the President* , 1994; U.S. Department of Labor, 1988

There has never been any doubt in my mind as to which route is preferable. It is really a matter of human dignity. Nobody should be forced to rely on subsidies and handouts. Yet if the incomes attached to some jobs are below the subsistence level, there is no other choice. Happily, the preferred solution is also the most economic, i.e. to raise minimum wages faster than the general rate for wage settlements. By raising the bottom group a little more, and the top group a little less, the total will equal the total increase in output and there will be no inflationary effect.

Again, exceptions are in order.   The object of the exercise is to increase the self-reliance of the working poor, and reduce their dependence on food stamps and subsidies which are a bureaucratically inefficient and costly way of redistributing income.   So exemptions can be granted for groups whose wages are not normally the only source of support.   The groups are students, who have not yet become full-time members of the labor force, senior citizens past retirement age who usually have pension income plus personal savings as core income, and disabled or disadvantaged persons entitled to income at some level on that account.   These three categories would provide a substantial market from which to fill marginal jobs at wages below the subsistence level.

The U.S. needs a substantial income redistribution in favor of the poor to compensate for the extra burden placed on their backs by the monetarist counter-revolution.   More money must find its way into the hands of people who will spend it for food, clothing and shelter which will stimulate the real economy.   A substantial redistribution is in the enlightened best interests of rich and poor alike.   When minimum wages are high enough to provide a standard of living equal to or better than welfare there is an inducement to work.   The opposite, it must be admitted, is equally true.

CONSTITUTIONAL AMENDMENTS

While a number of ideas discussed above are primarily to stimulate debate there are a couple of additional concerns I would like to address before returning to the five essential reforms.   As a Canadian I am particularly sensitive to the delicacy surrounding constitutional amendments, so it is a minefield I prefer to avoid; but if there were extreme nervousness about government reclaiming its right to create part or all of the increase in the money stock, objectors might be placated by a constitutional safeguard to the effect that the increase in any one year could not, under any circumstances, be more than proportional to the increase in real output for the preceding year, adjusted for the velocity of circulation and forecast changes in the size of the labor force. The provision could only be set aside by a seventy-five percent vote in both the Senate and the House of Representatives. The escape clause would never be used with the possible exception of a wartime emergency.

There is even less reason for a constitutional amendment requiring that the federal government budget be balanced. To achieve this goal will not be easy with existing economic policy. Even the adoption of a budget which separates capital expenditures from operating expense, always a sound accounting practice, would not paper over the deficiencies in the system. Monetary reform and the imposition of a few recommended taxes, however, would make it easy to operate at a surplus. The flexibility flowing from government-created money should make it possible for governments at all levels to balance their budgets – with or without a constitutional rule to that effect.

ELECTORAL REFORM

While I have proposed a number of reforms that I consider essential for the U.S. economy I have often wondered if any significant reform is really possible in the absence of electoral reform. U.S. politicians are far too dependent on the funding of special interest groups to be crusaders for ideas that would be vigorously opposed by some of them.

A couple of years ago I watched Bill Moyers' production "Corruption in U.S. Politics" on the Public Broadcasting System. It portrayed, in alarming reality, the influence of special interest groups on American politics. I recommend that every U.S. Senator and Congressman get a copy and watch it twice in order to understand the perception of outsiders concerning the political process. I have already affirmed that in my opinion politicians are no more or less corrupt than the people who elect them. But to put anyone, even the most honest of individuals, in the position where he or she is dependent on others for such vast amounts of money must inevitably affect their objectivity.

Adopting a system which reduces this dependence has to be in the public interest. Yes, public financing should be part of the electoral reform package. In the long run it would be more economical for taxpayers to pick up part of the tab once than to risk the possibility of paying indirectly several times over. I say this as an old politician who once thought that such reforms were unnecessary. I was wrong; and I would strongly urge my U.S. friends to face the reality of an existing system which makes significant legislative reform difficult bordering on impossible in several critical areas of greatest concern to the average American.

IN SUMMATION

In summation it should be said that the course being set by the U.S. Congress (not exclusive to the U.S.) is 180 degrees from common sense. I say this despite the double-page advertisements which appeared in *The New York Times* and *Wall Street Journal* on December 19, 1995, in which 91 top American businessmen urged the President and Congress to agree on a deficit reduction schedule to achieve a balanced budget within seven years. I don't doubt the sincerity of these men but I do wonder aloud if they really understand the difference between running a business and running a country. Most of the businessmen I know fail to make a distinction even though, in my opinion, the difference is profound – as I have inferred in this book.

In a slow growth economy further cuts by government will slow the economy even more. The policy being pursued is the policy of the mid-1930s. It has been totally discredited in the light of subsequent events and is every bit as inappropriate now as it was then. Radical reform is required – even more radical than was necessary to end the Great Depression and finance World War II.

There are five essential reforms. First, and of bedrock importance, is monetary reform. The government has to re-enter the money-creation business in a major way. There is no other acceptable means by which it can either maintain or increase government spending without increasing its deficit and going further into   debt.   Yet a high level of government expenditures is required to maintain economic growth at an acceptable level and the extra funds required should be debt-free government-created money.

Equally important to the long-term stability of the system is to put a cap on the total public and private debt to GDP ratio. There is no practical way this can be achieved if nearly all the new money created each year is created as debt. The only way the debt to GDP ratio can be capped is to inject into the system a substantial volume of debt-free money.

Capping the debt to GDP ratio also requires the re-instatement and maintenance of very low interest rates. Two essential reforms are required to make this possible. First, an incomes policy designed to produce very low inflation as a precursor to low interest rates. Second is the necessity of making central banks ultimately responsible to government to reduce the probability of another fledgling economic pilot getting his hands on the interest rate stick.

Tighter banking regulations are essential so that the money created by private banks is directed to increased output by productive enterprise, and to finance consumer expenditures, rather than such a large proportion being used for leveraged buyouts, takeovers, and speculation of all sorts by the financial services industry.

Finally, foreign exchange transactions must be taxed to the extent necessary to virtually eliminate short-term currency speculation so that governments can regain the independence necessary to operate their economies in the interests of their electors.

These, then, are the essentials. Monetary reform to stimulate the economy, reduce the deficit and help cap the total debt to income ratio; an incomes policy for monopolies and oligopolies to end significant inflation and pave the way for the low interest rates essential to both economic growth and capping the debt; tighter banking regulations to ensure that the money that is created privately is used in a way consistent with the public trust that a licence to "print" money really is; central banks must ultimately be accountable to government because democratic creativity is impossible in the face of absolute and unaccountable power; and foreign exchange transactions must be taxed to the extent necessary to restore some semblance of power and authority to democratically elected national governments.

These five reforms would turn the ship of state a full 180 degrees back in the direction of common sense, permit full employment and reasonable growth rates which, combined with the advantages of government-created money, lower interest on the public debt and increased tax revenue from foreign exchange transactions, would allow the treasury to budget for a surplus within two or three years and start paying down the federal debt instead of worrying about the statutory limit.

POSTSCRIPT

A STAR TO STEER BY

"Like the spider, there are those of us who refuse to stop spinning, even when it would appear to be far more sophisticated to be without hope. Our rope, though perhaps frail, can still be spun with optimism, curiosity, wonder, love, and the sincere desire to share a trip to the stars. Our goal is worth the struggle, for in this case the star to which we aspire is full humanity for all."

Leo F. Buscaglia

Until a couple of years ago when people asked me to name the number one problem in Canada I would reply "the economy" without a moment's hesitation. Then I began to reflect on what I was saying and slowly but surely came to a different conclusion. The number one problem is the moral and spiritual breakdown of our society. The same conclusion would appear to be equally valid for the United States and the rest of the Western World which is floating in a sea of self-indulgence like a ship without a rudder.

That doesn't mean that our economies aren't in the pits, as I have tried to make painfully clear. They are; but their condition is a symptom of the larger disease. They are what they are as a result of individual, collective and corporate greed and indifference towards the needs of others.

It is easy to blame politicians for the sad state of affairs but that is a classic example of passing the buck. Admittedly there are few saints in the political world, and this scribe is certainly no exception. But not everyone is willing to admit

193

that politicians' weaknesses and failures are a mirror of society. In the summer of 1992, on a day when Canada's provincial premiers were meeting in a last ditch effort to reach agreement on constitutional amendments, a lady who lives in the same condominium stopped me on the street and asked what I thought the news was likely to be that night. In the course of the discussion she launched into a diatribe against politicians which concluded with the affirmation that they are all a bunch of crooks. She only paused in mid-flight long enough to say – when she suddenly remembered what I had been doing most of my life – that in her opinion I was the sole exception. For my part I felt obliged to remind her that politicians are, on balance, a cross-section of the people who elect them.

There is no doubt in my mind that the ethical crisis is not limited to the body politic. It extends to the population as a whole. I was reminded of this when I took a close look at a Federal Reserve note. I have no doubt that there was a time when the Fathers of the Republic could honestly say "In God we Trust"; but as an outside, though friendly, observer I suspect that for the most part that time has long since gone. Today it would appear more appropriate for the U.S. currency to bear the inscription "In Power and Technology we Trust". In saying that I am aware that the U.S. ranks splendidly as a church-going nation. However, as is the case in Canada, a great part of that is habit and social custom. As a generator of social change and as an example of moral rectitude the roaring fire of faith of the pilgrim fathers appears to have been reduced to a few hot coals.

The United States can be rightfully proud of its achievement in space and landing the first man on the moon. If it had spent one-tenth of one-percent as much scientific effort and brainpower on the problems of unemployment and poverty, and just a fraction of the cost of the space program in implementation, the ideas contained in this book would have been overtaken by time years ago. Instead we seem to be moving from bad to worse. As Milton Friedman and Anna Jacobson Schwartz point out in *A Monetary History of the United States 1867-1960*, the Fed could have taken action to mitigate the severity of the Great Depression of the 1930s which devastated the whole Western world.[1] Instead it took a devastating war to accomplish what our financial leaders were incapable of accomplishing. Following that dreadful war we enjoyed 20 years of prosperity – the longest stretch in the history of capitalism. The party could have lasted much longer had the most powerful members of society been content with fair shares. But that was not the case and when this excess was confronted by the monetarist "theology" it resulted in stagflation and then the two most disastrous recessions since the 1930s.

Each time the U.S. economy has slumped the consequences have been far-reaching. In 1930 the introduction of the Smoot-Hawley bill, with its protectionist stance, slowed the recovery process immeasurably.[2] Today the U.S. is a champion of free trade, but more in theory than in practice. In practice it uses U.S. law to frustrate free exchange and indulges in practices that range from tough to almost brutal. All of this in the name of protecting U.S. jobs and U.S. interests at a time when both of these are primarily the victim of U.S. domestic economic policy.

It seems to me, therefore, that any treatise on economics is incomplete without an attempt to put it in a philosophical context. We have already concluded that a privately-administered, decentralized system is the most productive. Individuals will work harder if they know that there will be rewards for their effort. Questions that remain include the means by which the maximum number of individuals will be allowed to participate, the limits between opportunity and exploitation, and the extent to which stewardship involves sharing with other members of the family of man.

It was especially fitting that 1994 should be both the UN International Year of the Family and the 50th Anniversary of D-Day, the invasion of Normandy by the most massive sea-launched military offensive in history. Allied veterans by the thousands returned on June 6th to those beaches which meant death to so many and hope to even greater numbers of those being liberated. So there were mixed emotions as they met for services of remembrance followed by dancing on the streets and reminiscing in the pubs.

It is easy to romanticize what the soldiers, sailors and airmen fought and died for. Perhaps some of them didn't even know. But most of the veterans who lived to express themselves say that they fought that men and women everywhere might be free – free to follow their own pursuits without fear, harassment or oppression. When pressed they admit that they did not risk their lives just to maintain the freedoms of speech, religion and expression; they thought it would be a world of justice, where people who wanted to work would be able to get jobs and where there would be freedom from poverty and homelessness.

The United Nations International Year of the Family was a timely reminder that our responsibilities extend beyond ourselves. A set of stamps beautifully designed by UN staff member Rocco J. Callari portrayed the common themes against a common background of the International Year of the Family emblem – a heart sheltered by a roof and linked to another heart. The common background design was meant to symbolize life and love within a home. Each stamp had a different superimposed theme including the concept of inter-generational equality, responsible fatherhood, poverty in families, the value of the extended family, regional and international action on behalf of families and partnership in domestic responsibilities – struggles that are as ongoing as time itself.

Man has always looked for meaning in life beyond day-to-day struggles for existence. It is not by accident, then, that most North Americans admit at least token allegiance to one of the great religions of the world. What is more surprising is the extent to which there are common threads when it comes to questions such as sharing and responsibility for those members of society that are less well off than ourselves.

Both the Protestant and Catholic branches of the Christian church profess deep concern for the poor, the incapacitated and the disadvantaged. The great Archbishop of Canterbury, William Temple (1881-1944), once said that the church of Jesus Christ is the only cooperative society that exists for the benefit of its non-members.

This is in contrast to "the view that would limit the Church's action today, as always, to what is 'spiritual', and contends that it must, as far as possible, keep itself from involvement and contamination in the affairs of 'the world.'" "This", as a commission of the Church of Scotland goes on to say, "is quite unrealistic, comes near to being a form of religious escapism, and is based on a quite unscriptural idea of spirituality. It is, besides, false to the authentic record of the ministry and teaching of Christ, who spent a considerable part of His time healing men's bodies and made clear, in some of His parables and in His picture of the Last Judgment, that the final testing of men is in a very real way bound up with what they have done in the world to feed the hungry, clothe the naked, befriend the stranger, visit the sick and the prisoner. There is not a page of the New Testament but makes clear that practical ways of loving one's neighbour are an integral part of faith in God."[3] "He that loveth not his brother whom he hath seen, how can he love God whom he hath not seen."[4]

Robert J. Keller, O.P., whose doctoral dissertation is on Roman Catholic theology, says: "At the heart of a Catholic theological and philosophical understanding of the economy is the human person as agent, and more specifically, as worker. Humans bear the image of God, the Creator, therefore, we share in the imaginative activity of creating a world out of our labors.

"The source of economy is productive work. The Catholic tradition has long held that property, the product of work, belongs to its creator: the worker. This ownership, whether individual or collective, is never absolute; only God possesses the world. All property, goods, and ownership are measured by the welfare of the common good. Thus, economy is evaluated by what it does **for** people, **to** people, and how each one **participates** in it. At the very least, work is the means whereby persons provide basic sustenance for themselves and their families. Economic structures which explicitly or implicitly stifle this familial duty are unjust."[5]

The Reverend Friar continues: "Solidarity is a social virtue derived from the gospel demand to love each and all.

When the demands of love appeal to justice for the most vulnerable and disadvantaged, the Church's social teaching speaks of an 'option for the poor.' In short, economy is a playing field of Christian love and justice, and the workaday world is the complement of the work of worship: liturgy."[6]

When I asked my good friend Rabbi David Monson, Rabbi Emeritus of Beth Sholom Synagogue, in Toronto, concerning Judaism's position in these matters he referred me to excerpts from Charity in Judaism. I must admit some surprise when I found that: "There is no word in the Hebrew language that really expresses the term 'Charity' as we know it. The Hebrew word that we use, Tzedaka, really means 'righteousness' and not 'Charity'.

"Why is this so?

"Simply because in Judaism there is a beautiful attitude toward the whole problem of giving alms to the poor. When you give to a needy person, you are doing only what is expected of you. You are doing the right thing. Judaism teaches us that it is a 'Mitzvah – *commandment*' to give aid where it is needed. It is not a matter of personal choice with us. On the contrary, we are obliged to share with those who are less fortunate than we. That is why the Hebrew language has no literal word for Charity. Whether we are rich or poor, great or small, high or lowly, we owe our fellow men help and sympathy, love and kindness. We have no right to decline any call for aid. We *must* help. We are unrighteous if we do not give aid. That is why the Hebrew word is Tzedaka – Righteousness."[7]

Although the Qur'an does not talk about love in the way that both the Jewish Bible and the New Testament do, its implied consequences of community and caring are fundamental to Islamic law. According to Jane I. Smith, Vice President and Dean of Academic Affairs, Iliff School of Theology, "The notion of responsibility to others is essential in Islam. It pervades the Qur'an, suggesting that one has the responsibility to care for the poor, for women, for widows and orphans, for strangers, and for any other people with needs. One of the five major responsibilities incumbent upon all Muslims is paying the almstax (zakat), which is roughly equivalent to a tithe. The reason for this is so that those who are needy can be taken care of. Sacrifice of animals at the major festival times is so that the meat of the animal sacrificed can be shared with the poor. There are many examples of this kind of concern. And it is clear that when one is judged at the day of the resurrection one of the elements of that judgment will be the basis of the degree to which one carried out one's responsibility to others in the community...

"Muslims believe that God is just, and because that is so humans are called upon to act justly to their fellows. In that way they not only carry out a human responsibility designated by God, but by acting justly actually acknowledge justice as a quality of the divine."[8]

"The fundamental principle of Buddhist ethics is that all men should develop an attitude of compassion – a very highly esteemed virtue in Buddhism. True wisdom consists not in metaphysical sophistication but in practical knowledge expressed in compassion as the fundamental principle in social life. Compassion or love in Sanskrit is *maitrī* (Pāli *mettā*), derived from *mitra* (friend). Thus, the term embodies the meaning 'true friendliness'. If one allows the virtue of compassion or love to grow in him, it will not occur to him to harm anyone else any more than he would willingly harm himself. By widening the boundaries of what one regards as his own, he breaks down the barriers that separate him from others."[9]

The ethical values of North American Aboriginal peoples include a sense of community, responsibility for other members of the tribe and a deep attachment to the earth which is considered almost holy. "Morals set the limits and boundaries of personal behavior and ethics teach social behavior or the way individuals order their behavior with one another... By understanding ecological relationships and taking care to maintain them and learn from them, human beings maintain their own lives. We have also seen that North American sacred oral traditions teach people that they are dependent on each other and on many predictable and unpredictable things in the world.

"In Native communities, the moral and ethical behavior that was taught was really behavior that was necessary for survival in the natural world. The individual was taught to be responsible for his or herself but not in isolation from the rest of the community."[10]

When the basic philosophies of the vast majority of North Americans include belief in the dignity of work, the need for justice, the exercise of compassion and concern for one's neighbors you have to wonder how we managed to get our work-day practices so screwed up. Is there any justice in the fact that millions of people are unemployed involuntarily – and quite unnecessarily? Is it morally acceptable for people with monopoly power to use it in a way that contributes to the high level of unemployment? Is it right that some of the highest paid and most secure members of society should deliberately cause recessions that hurt and humiliate millions of the poorer and weaker members of society? And what is the moral judgment of economic policies that reduce the creation of wealth by trillions of dollars when there are needy outstretched hands from one corner of the globe to the other?

When I was writing about this subject in 1990 I was informed that one of every four children born in the Third World will die before the age of five. In one year there will be 7.6 million deaths from impure water. Another 3.5 million will die from communicable diseases. One-third of these are from diseases like whooping cough, diphtheria, tuberculosis and other diseases that are almost extinct in the United States and Canada.

The figure of 10.6 million deaths is so large that it is almost beyond comprehension. An illustration helps put it in context. We were all shocked a few years ago when a Korean 747 jet was shot down and all the crew and passengers killed; and in a subsequent disaster, when a Pan Am flight was blown out of the air over Lockerbie, Scotland. These were dreadful tragedies that attracted widespread and prolonged attention. Yet the number of children dying needlessly each year from impure water and lack of immunization is the equivalent of one Boeing 747 carrying 360 passengers being shot down every 18 minutes, day and night, 365 days a year. If these hypothetical planes were filled with American kids or Canadian, English, French or German, someone would move heaven and earth to do something about it. Some progress is being made but it's at a snail's pace. The world's indifference is called the silent tragedy.

If this all sounds a little preachy I suppose that is fair comment but less so in the context of its wider meaning. I am not one who draws a clear distinction between moral law and enlightened self-interest. When Moses delivered the Ten Commandments he may have hoped that they would put the fear of the Lord into the hearts of the Children of Israel. But another interpretation of the decalogue might be that it reflects the wisdom of a loving parent who says: "My children, to the extent that you are able to live according to these precepts you will save yourselves a lot of grief."

I believe that the way we have operated our economies for the last couple of decades, and the way we continue to operate them, fails just about any test of morality or common sense that could be applied. The flip-side of the coin is that we have caused ourselves a lot of unnecessary grief in lives ruined, families broken up, dreams shattered and opportunities lost. We have been sowing the wind and reaping the whirlwind.

The whirlwind we are reaping is a kind of casino mentality, both literally and figuratively. Periodic recessions reduce the revenues of states and provinces so they look to lotteries and casinos for extra revenue. First Nations' bands are faced with inadequate job opportunities for their members so they turn to casinos for jobs and revenue. The banks find the pickings from their traditional business a little thin so they start writing derivatives which create new and uncertain risks. As Henry Kaufman said in a talk delivered before the City of London Conference on Derivatives, in October 1993, "If, as many in senior management maintain, the bulk of the profits comes from 'running the casino' rather than 'playing at the tables', that should be backed up with hard numbers. Otherwise, the suspicion is that profits stem mainly from position-taking, which entails market exposure, and not from merely marrying bids and offers."[11]

This kind of activity has one thing in common – for

every winner there is a loser. Contrast this with activity that creates real wealth which is a win-win situation for investor, worker and tax-collectors alike. Surely the object of a just, caring society should be to allow everyone to accumulate a little stake rather than to "clean their clock". Most people don't ask for the mansions and conspicuous consumption of the rich. The majority, especially the poor, would settle for the five basics which include adequate food, clothing, shelter, telephone and television. Millions in the Third World would settle for much less.

So the options are clear. We can continue on the present course until the financial super-structure crashes all around us with earth-shattering consequences for millions, or we can reform the system in a way that will provide stability and opportunity. Even then, however, the kind of society that most of us dream of will not come automatically. The mess we're in is a result of the attitudes and actions of men and women. We are responsible for the failure of the system to meet the needs and aspirations of the unhappy minority. Even a reformed system will not achieve its potential unless good men and women make it work well. The policies recommended in this book are a good place to start.

One cannot fail to be concerned about generation X, the millions of young people who are being led to believe that the future will be less bright for them than it was for their parents. My message of hope for them is that the future is in their hands if they are willing to grasp the torch of truth and hold it high. They can run for public office to participate in the implementation of the essential reforms. Or, failing that, they can gently but resolutely refuse to vote for anyone who is not committed to fundamental change.

The U.S. economy and, by extension, the World economy can only achieve its potential as a result of a revolutionary change of heart and mind on the part of the people who manage it. Generation X will have to translate the lip-service their elders pay to honesty, justice and compassion into the reality of the marketplace. Some would call it the moral thing to do; others would just say it is the essence of common sense.

NOTES

Chapter 1: Monetarists and the Chicago School Blew It!

1. Kaufman, Henry, in Morgello, Clem, *Institutional Investor*, June 1987. This copyrighted material is reprinted with permission from Institutional Investor.
2. Solomon, Steven, *The Confidence Game: How Unelected Central Bankers Are Governing the Changed Global Economy*, New York: Simon & Schuster, 1995, p. 149.
3. *Ibid*, p. 508.
4. Bartley, Robert L., "Giving Up on Growth", *The Wall Street Journal*, September 13, 1995.
5. Courtesy of Professor Wallace Peterson, George Holmes Professor of Economics Emeritus, University of Nebraska – Lincoln.
6. Passell, Peter, "A Nobel Award for a University of Chicago Economist, Yet Again". Copyright © 1995, October 11, p. C1, by *The New York Times Company*. Reprinted by permission.

Chapter 2: Where Mainline Economists Went Wrong

1. Friedman, Milton, *Monetarist Economics*, Oxford: Basil Blackwell Ltd., 1991, pp. 14-18. Reprinted by permission of Blackwell Publishers.
2. *Ibid.*, p. 16.
3. *Ibid.*, p 13.
4. Bladen, Vincent, "Prescribing Remedies for Inflation", *The Globe and Mail*, August 29, 1973.
5. Lekachman, Robert, *Inflation: The Permanent Problem of Boom and Bust*, New York: Vintage Books, 1973, p. 37.
6. *Annual Report of the Council of Economic Advisers*, Washington, D.C., January 1981, p. 39.
7. Samuelson, Paul A., *Economics*, 9th ed., New York: McGraw-Hill Book Co., 1973, p. 829. Reprinted by permission.
8. *Bank of Canada Annual Report*, February 27, 1981, p. 16.
9. O.E.C.D. Main Economic Indicators, 1965-70.
10. *Economic Report of the President*, January 1981, pp. 7-8.
11. *Ibid.*, p. 8.
12. *Ibid.*
13 Friedman, Milton, *A Program for Monetary Stability*, New York: Fordham University Press, 1959.
14. The letter was written by John Crispo and Douglas Hartle of the University of Toronto and signed by all seventeen.
15. Harriss, C. Lowell, "Causes and Effects of Inflation", *Inflation: Long-Term Problems*, New York: The Academy of Political Science, 1975, pp. 11-12.
16. *Ibid.*

17.   *Annual Report of the Council of Economic Advisers*, February 1982, pp. 95-96.
18.   *Ibid.*, p. 95.
19.   Crozier, Robert B., *Deficit Financing and Inflation: Facts and Fictions*, The Conference Board of Canada, March 1976.
20.   *Economic Report of the President*, January 1981, pp. 41-42.
21.   *Annual Report of the Council of Economic Advisers*, February 1982, p. 99.
22.   Harriss, C. Lowell, *Inflation: Long-Term Problems*, op. cit., pp. 11-12.
23.   *Congressional Quarterly*, 1975, p. 14.
24.   *Ibid.*
25.   *Ibid.*
26.   *Economic Report of the President*, January 1980, p. 3.
27.   *Annual Report of the Council of Economic Advisers*, February 1983, p. 225.
28.   Mundell, Robert A., Professor of Economics at Cambridge, and Arthur B. Laffer, then of the University of Chicago Graduate School of Business.
29.   *Bank of Canada Annual Report*, Ottawa, March 1981, p. 11.

Chapter 3: The Schizo Economy

1.   1982 Census of Manufacturers, *Concentration Ratios in Manufacturing*, Washington D.C.: U.S. Department of Commerce, 1985.
2.   Stigler, George J., "Monopoly & Oligopoly by Merger", *American Economic Review Supplement*, XL, 1950, p. 23 ff.
3.   Low, Richard E. (ed.), *The Economics of Antitrust: Competition and Monopoly*, Englewood Cliffs: Prentice-Hall Inc., 1968, p. 6.
4.   Caves, Richard E., *American Industry: Structure, Conduct, Performance*, 7th ed. Englewood Cliffs: Prentice-Hall Inc., 1992, p. 51.
5.   Munkirs, John R., *The Transformation of American Capitalism From Competitive Market Structures to Centralized Private Sector Planning*, New York: M.E. Sharpe, Inc., 1985.
6.   Reynolds, Morgan O., "Labor Unions", *The Fortune Encyclopedia of Economics*, Henderson, David R. (ed.), New York: Warner Books, Inc., 1993, p. 494.
7.   *Ibid.*
8.   Jones, Aubrey, *The New Inflation: The Politics of Prices and Incomes*, London: Andre Deutsch, 1973.
9.   McCarthy, W.E.J.; O'Brien, J.F., and V.G. Dowd, *Wage Inflation and Wage Leadership: A Study of the Role of Key Wage Bargains in the Irish System of Collective Bargaining*, Dublin: Cahill & Co. Ltd., 1975, p. 11.

10. *Annual Report of the Council of Economic Advisers*, Washington, D.C., January 1981, p. 34.

11. Source: Q,W – OECD National Accounts; P=CPI in IMF International Financial Statistics; Labor Force – OECD Labor Force Statistics.

12. Friedman, Milton, and Friedman, Rose D., *Free to Choose: A Personal Statement*, New York: Harcourt Brace Jovanovich, Inc., 1981, p. 11.

13. Weintraub, Sidney, *Capitalism's Inflation and Unemployment Crisis: Beyond Monetarism and Keynesiasm*, ©1978 Addison-Wesley Publishing Company, Inc., p. 104. Reprinted by permission of Addison-Wesley Publishing Company, Inc.

14. Friedman, Milton, and Friedman, Rose D., *Free to Choose: A Personal Statement*, op. cit., p. 251.

Chapter 4: Light on the Horizon

1. Editorial, "Across the Great Divide", *The Wall Street Journal*, October 2, 1995, p. A14.

2. Hellyer, Paul, *Exit Inflation*, Toronto: Nelson Canada Limited, 1981, p. 9.

3. Sources: Informetrica Limited, and Statistics Canada.

4. Sources: Laurence H. Meyer & Associates, Limited, and Informetrica Limited.

Chapter 5: Money, Funny Money and Phantom Money

1. Holy Bible, The New King James Version, Thomas Nelson Inc., 1983, Genesis 47, Verses 13-17, p. 48.

2. Lui, Francis T., "Cagan's Hypothesis and the First Nationwide Inflation of Paper Money in World History", *Major Inflations in History*, Capie, Forrest H. (ed.), Aldershot: Edward Elgar Publishing Ltd., 1991, pp. 210-212.

3. *Ibid.*

4. Chaffers, William, *Gilda Aurifabrorum: A History of English Goldsmiths and Plateworkers, and Their Marks Stamped on Plate*, London: Reeves & Turner, [1800], p. 210.

5. *Ibid.*

6. Hixson, William F., *Triumph of the Bankers: Money and Banking in the Eighteenth and Nineteenth Centuries*, Westport: Praeger Publishers, 1993, p. 46.

7. *Ibid*, p. 60.

8. Nettles, Curtis P., *The Money Supply of the American Colonies before 1720*, New York: Augustus M. Kelley, 1964, p. 169.

9. Powell, Ellis T., *The Evolution of the Money Market – 1385-1915*, New York: Augustus M. Kelley, 1966, p. 197.

10. *Ibid.*, pp. 117-118.
11. *Ibid.*, p. 129.
12. Innis, Mary Quayle, *An Economic History of Canada*, Toronto: The Ryerson Press, 1935, p. 28.
13. Lester, Richard A., "Currency Issues to Overcome Depressions in Pennsylvania, 1723 and 1729", *The Journal of Political Economy*, Vol. 46, June 1938, p. 326.
14. Hixson, William F., *Triumph of the Bankers*, op. cit., p. 46.
15. Lester, Richard A., *The Journal of Political Economy*, op. cit., p. 338.
16. *Ibid.*, p. 341.
17. Smith, Adam, *Wealth of Nations*, New York: P.F. Collier and Son, 1909, p. 266.
18. Nettles, Curtis P., *The Money Supply of the American Colonies before 1720*, op. cit., p. 265.
19. Ferguson, E. James, *The Power of the Purse: A History of American Public Finance, 1776-1790*, Chapel Hill: University of North Carolina Press, 1961, p. 16.
20. Hixson, William F., *Triumph of the Bankers*, op. cit., p. 81.
21. Franklin, Benjamin, *The Writings of Benjamin Franklin*, Smyth, Albert Henry (ed.), New York: Macmillan, 1907, (9), pp. 231-233.
22. Hixson, William F., *Triumph of the Bankers*, op. cit., p. 80.
23. *Ibid.*
24. Morris, Richard B., *The Forging of the Union 1781-1789*, New York: Harper & Row, 1987, p. 155.
25. Hixson, William F., *Triumph of the Bankers*, op. cit., p. 115.
26. Sumner, William Graham, *A History of American Currency*, New York: Augustus M. Kelley, 1968, p. 123.
27. Gouge, William M., *A Short History of Paper Money and Banking in the United States*, New York: Augustus M. Kelley, Part II, 1968, p. 45.
28. Angell, Norman, *The Story of Money*, New York: Frederick A. Stokes Co., 1929, p. 294.
29. Hixson, William, F., *Triumph of the Bankers*, op. cit., p. 150.
30. Bordo, Michael D., "Gold Standard", *The Fortune Encyclopedia of Economics*, Henderson, David R. (ed.), New York: Warner Books, Inc., 1993, p. 359.
31. *Ibid.*
32. For budget discussion see U.K. Parliamentary Debates, Vol. clxxxiii, col. 55.
33. *Ibid.*
34. Bordo, Michael D., *The Fortune Encyclopedia of Economics*, op. cit., p. 360.
35. Galbraith, John Kenneth, *Money, Whence it Came, Where it Went*, Boston: Houghton Mifflin Company, 1975, pp. 10-11.

Chapter 6: Phantom Money Reigns Supreme

1.   Stiglitz, Joseph E., "Information", *The Fortune Encyclopedia of Economics*, Henderson, David R. (ed.), New York: Warner Books, Inc., 1993, p. 18.
2.   Schwartz, Anna J., "Money Supply", *The Fortune Encyclopedia of Economics*, Henderson, David R. (ed.), New York: Warner Books, Inc., 1993, p. 365.
3.   *Seventy-Ninth Annual Report of the Board of Governors of the Federal Reserve System*, 1992, p. 281.
4.   Source: IMF – International Financial Statistics, 1993, 1995.
5.   Saul, John Ralston, *Voltaire's Bastards: The Dictatorship of Reason in the West*. Copyright © John Ralston Saul, 1992, pp. 376-377. Reprinted by permission of Penguin Books Canada Limited.
6.   Strom, Stephanie, "This Year's Wave of Mergers Heads Toward A Record", *The New York Times*, October 3, 1995, p. A1
7.   *Ibid.*
8.   Article, "U.S. mergers reach record high", *The Globe and Mail*, September 30, 1995, p. B5.
9.   *The State of the World's Children, 1992, Summary*, New York: Oxford University Press, pp. 8-11.
10.   *Ibid.*
11.   "You'd better ask Murphy", *The Banker*, February 1993, p. 48.
12.   Samuelson, Robert J., "Great Depression", *The Fortune Encyclopedia of Economics*, Henderson, David R. (ed.), New York: Warner Books, Inc., 1993, p. 202.

Chapter 7: An Infinitely Silly System

1.   Hixson, William F., *Triumph of the Bankers: Money and Banking in the Eighteenth and Nineteenth Centuries*, Westport: Praeger Publishers, 1993, p. 81.
2.   *Ibid.*, pp. 45-58.
3.   Metcalf, Jack, *The Two Hundred Year Debate: Who Shall Issue the Nation's Money*, Olympia: An Honest Money for America Publication, 1986, p. 91.
4.   *Ibid.*
5.   *Ibid*, p. 92.
6.   Lux, Kenneth, *Adam Smith's Mistake: How a Moral Philosopher Invented Economics and Ended Morality*, Boston: Shambhala Publications, Inc., 1990, p. 76.
7.   Friedman, Milton and Schwartz, Anna Jacobson, *A Monetary History of the United States 1867-1960*, Princeton: Princeton University Press, 1963, p. 322.
8.   Day, Donald, *Will Rogers: A Biography*, New York: David McKay Company, Inc., 1962, p. 285.

9. Friedman, Milton and Schwartz, Anna Jacobson, *A Monetary History of the United States 1867-1960*, op. cit.

10. *Ibid.*, pp. 327-328.

11. *Maclean's Magazine*, July 1, 1933 as reprinted in *The Journal of Economic History*, Goldin, Claudia, and Hohenberg, Paul (eds.), The Economic History Association, University of Pennsylvania, June 1987, Vol. XLVII, No. 2, p. 415.

12. Volcker, Paul A., Statement by Chairman, Board of Governors of the Federal Reserve System, before the Joint Economic Committee of the U.S. Congress, January 26, 1982.

13. Friedman, Milton, "A Second Industrial Revolution", speech given at the 9th Dr. Harold Walter Siebens Lecture, The Fraser Institute, Vancouver, B.C., May 18, 1994.

14. Cooper, Richard N., "A Monetary System for the Future", *Foreign Affairs*, Vol. 63, #1, Fall 1984, pp. 166-184.

Chapter 8: Re-Inventing the Wheel

1. Friedman, Milton, "A Monetary and Fiscal Framework for Economic Stability", *American Economic Review*, XXXVIII, June 1948.

2. Friedman, Milton, *A Program for Monetary Stability*, New York: Fordham University Press, 1959, p. 65.

3. *Ibid.* Henry C. Simons, "A Positive Program for Laissez Faire: Some Proposals for a Liberal Economic Policy," in *Economic Policy for A Free Society* (Chicago, 1948), pp. 62-5 (first published as Public Policy Pamphlet, No. 15, ed. Harry D. Gideonse (Chicago, 1934); Lloyd W. Mints, *Monetary Policy for a Competitive Society* (New York, 1950), pp. 186-87. Albert G. Hart, "The 'Chicago Plan' of Banking Reform", *Review of Economic Studies*, 2 (1935), pp. 104-16. Reprinted in Friedrich A. Lutz and Lloyd W. Mints (eds.), *Readings in Monetary Theory* (New York, 1951), pp. 437-56.

4. Fisher, Irving, *100% Money*, New York: The Adelphi Company, 1935.

5. Hixson, William F., *Triumph of the Bankers: Money and Banking in the Eighteenth and Nineteenth Centuries*, Westport: Praeger Publishers, 1993, p. 49.

6. Nicolay, John G., and Hay, John (eds.), *Abraham Lincoln: Complete Works*, New York: The Century Co., 1907, 2: p. 264.

7. Hixson, William F., *Triumph of the Bankers*, op. cit., p. 134.

8. Hammond, Bray, *Sovereignty and an Empty Purse*, Princeton: Princeton University Press, 1970, p. 192.

9. Campbell, Alexander, *The True Greenback*, Chicago: Republican Books, 1868, p. 31.

10. McCulloch, Hugh, *Men and Measures of Half a Century*, New York: Charles Scribner's Sons, 1888, p. 201.

11. Myers, Margaret G., *A Financial History of the United States*, New York: Columbia University Press, 1970, p. 198.

12. McPherson, Edward (ed.), *A Handbook of Politics*, New York: Da Capo Publishing Corp., 1972, p. 271.

13. Low, Solon E., *Hansard*, Vol. 2, 5th Session, March 10, 1949, p. 1334.

14. Blackmore, John H., *Hansard*, Vol. 6, 3rd Session, July 24, 1956, p. 6368.

15. Confirmed in telephone conversation with Robert Thompson on July 7, 1994.

16. McIvor, R. Craig, *Canadian Monetary, Banking and Fiscal Development*, Toronto: The Macmillan Company of Canada Limited, 1958, p. 160.

17. Simons, Henry C., *Economic Policy for a Free Society*, Chicago: University of Chicago Press, 1948, pp. 65-66.

18. Phillips, Ronnie J., *The Chicago Plan & New Deal Banking Reform*, New York: M.E. Sharpe, Inc., 1995, pp. 47-48.

19. Simons, Henry C., *Economic Policy for a Free Society*, op. cit., p. 80.

20. Cameron, Duncan and Finn, Ed, *Ten Debt/Deficit Myths*, Ottawa: Canadian Centre for Policy Alternatives, 1996.

21. Grant, Jordan B., *Reintegrating Monetary Policy Into the Economic Tool Kit*, January 24, 1994.

22. Information provided by Professor John H. Hotson, Executive Director, The Committee on Monetary and Economic Reform, August 8, 1994.

23. Biddell, Jack L., *A Self-Reliant Future for Canada*, Thornhill: LNC Publications, 1993, p. 98.

24. DeGeer, Gerald Gratton, Mayor of Vancouver, Dec. 1934 for 2 years; Dec. 1946 for 2 years but passed away Aug. 1947.

25. Cowles, Virginia, *The Rothschilds: A Family of Fortune*, New York: Alfred A. Knopf, Inc., 1973.

26. *"Michael" Journal*, Quebec, July-August, 1994, p. 17.

27. Fisher, Irving, *100% Money*, op. cit., p. 20.

28. Friedman, Milton, *A Program For Monetary Stability*, op. cit., pp. 65-66.

29. *Ibid.*, p. 75.

Chapter 9: A 50% Solution

1. Chaffers, William, *Gilda Aurifabrorum: A History of English Goldsmiths and Plateworkers, and Their Marks Stamped on Plate*, London: Reeves & Turner, [1800], pp. 210-211.

2. *Ibid.*

3.   Fisher, Irving, *100% Money*, New York: The Adelphi Company, 1935, p. 8.
4.   *Ibid.*, pp. 10-12.
5.   Friedman, Milton, in a footnote reply to a letter from William F. Hixson, November 9, 1983.
6.   Friedman, Milton, in a letter to Professor John H. Hotson, February 3, 1986.
7.   *Ibid.*
8.   Sources: Laurence H. Meyer & Associates, Limited, and Informetrica Limited.
9.   Pope, William Henry, "The Value of the Dollar".

Chapter 10: An Incomes Policy for Monopolies and Oligopolies

1.   Passell, Peter, "Has This War Been Won?". Copyright © 1995, October 25, p. C1, C3, by *The New York Times Company*. Reprinted by permission.
2.   As recorded by me following a private conversation in February, 1966.
3.   *Economic Report of the President*, January 1979, p. 4.
4.   *Annual Report of the Council of Economic Advisers*, Washington, D.C., January 1979, p. 82.
5.   Decision by U.S. District Judge Barrington Parker, May 31, 1979.
6.   *Annual Report of the Council of Economic Advisers*, January 1980, pp. 36-38.
7.   *Ibid.*
8.   Mill, John Stuart, *Principles of Political Economy with some of their Applications to Social Philosophy*, New York: Augustus M. Kelley, 1909, p. 963.
9.   The prediction was stated in a press release issued by Action Canada.
10.   Galbraith, John Kenneth, *The New Industrial State*, Boston: Houghton Mifflin Co., 1971.
11.   On a $15,000 house.
12.   Wage drift is an arbitrary system of job reclassification that could nullify the intent of wage guidelines or controls.
13.   Lead Editorial, "Time for an Incomes Policy", *The New York Times*, May 5, 1983.
14.   *Annual Report of the Council of Economic Advisers*, January 1981, pp. 61-65.
15.   *Ibid.*
16.   *Ibid.*
17.   *Ibid.*
18.   Federal Reserve Bulletin, November 1995.

Chapter 11: Some Myths and Realities of Economics

1. Lux, Kenneth, *Adam Smith's Mistake: How a Moral Philosopher Invented Economics and Ended Morality*, Boston: Shambhala Publications Inc., 1990, p. 54.
2. Smith, Adam, *The Wealth of Nations*, Cannan, Edwin (ed.), New York: Modern Library, 1937, Book 1, Chapter 2, p. 14.
3. Galbraith, John Kenneth, *A Journey Through Economic Time: A Firsthand View*, New York: Houghton Mifflin Company, 1994, p. 47.
4. Schumacher, Ernst F., *Small is Beautiful: Economics as if People Mattered*, New York: Harper & Row, 1989, p. 2
5. Friedman, Milton, "A Second Industrial Revolution", speech given at the 9th Dr. Harold Walter Siebens Lecture, The Fraser Institute, Vancouver, B.C., May 18, 1994.
6. The OECD Jobs Study, "Facts-Analysis-Strategies, Unemployment in the OECD Area 1950-1995", Organization for Economic Co-operation and Development, 1994, p. 10.

Chapter 12: The Package of Economic Reforms

1. Haliechuk, Rick, "Deposit safety must come first: bank group chief", *The Toronto Star*, March 29, 1994, p. B3
2. *The Toronto Stock Exchange Fact Sheet*, "Findings of the TSE-ESOP Database", 1989.
3. Special, "Global Panic Spreads – And It Is Over the Economy, Stupid", *New Federalist*, April 6, 1994.
4. *Ibid.*
5. Gelder, Lawrence van, "After Merger, Chase to Shut 7 New York City Branches", *The New York Times*, September 22, 1995, p. C17.
6. Hirsch, James S., "Bank of Boston Wins Bid to Buy Boston Bancorp in a Stock Swap", *The Wall Street Journal*, October 12, 1995, p. B4.
7. By Bloomberg Business News, "Lloyds Bank Agrees To Merge With TSB", *The New York Times*, October 12, 1995, p. C17.
8. Article, "Teller, Beware", *Time Magazine*, September 11, 1995, p. 25.
9. Article, "Deutsche Bank Plan To Cut 10,000 Jobs", *The New York Times*, September 18, 1995, p. C2.
10. O'Brien, Timothy L., "On-Line Banking Has Bankers Fretting PCs May Replace Branches", *The Wall Street Journal*, October 25, 1995, p. A1, A13.
11. See *The Future of Retail Banking, A Global Perspective*, Deloitte & Touche Consulting Group, Deloitte Touche Tohmatsu International.
12. Tobin, James, "A Proposal for International Monetary Reform", *Eastern Economic Journal*, 1978, Vol. 4, pp. 154-155.

13. Felix, David, *Challenge*, May/June, 1995.
14. Halifax Summit, *Communiqué*, June 15-17, p. 1, 1995.
15. Millman, Gregory J., *Vandals' Crown: How Rebel Currency Traders Overthrew the World's Central Banks*, New York: The Free Press, 1995.
16. Canadian Broadcasting Corporation, "Sunday Morning: Economic Forecasting", September 24, 1995.
17. Deane, Marjorie, and Pringle, Robert, *The Central Banks*, London: Hamish Hamilton Ltd., 1994, p. vii.
18. Gorman, Linda, "Minimum Wages", *The Fortune Encyclopedia of Economics*, Henderson, David R. (ed.), New York: Warner Books, Inc., 1993, p. 449.
19. *Ibid.*

Postscript: A Star to Steer By

1. Friedman, Milton and Schwartz, Anna Jacobson, *A Monetary History of the United States 1867-1960*, Princeton: Princeton University Press, 1963.
2. The Smoot-Hawley Bill was enacted by Congress in 1930.
3. "The Church Faces the Challenge", The Report of the Church of Scotland Commission on Communism, London: Longmans, Green and Co. Ltd., 1955, p. 9.
4. Holy Bible, The New King James Version, Thomas Nelson Inc., 1983, I John, 4, Verse 20.
5. Keller, Robert J., O.P., PhD, Director of the Catholic (Newman) Center at Emory University, Atlanta, Georgia, in a letter to the author dated April 29, 1944.
6. *Ibid.*
7. Steinbach, Alexander Alan, *What is Judaism*, New York: Behrman Jewish Book House, 1937, p. 40.
8. Smith, Jane I., Vice President and Dean of Academic Affairs, Iliff School of Theology, Denver, Colorado, in a letter to the author dated April 20, 1994.
9. From "Buddhist Philosophy", *Encyclopaedia Britannica*, 15th ed., 3:429, 1981. Reprinted by permission of Encyclopaedia Britannica, Inc.
10. Beck, Peggy V. and Walters, Anna L., *The Sacred: Ways of Knowledge Sources of Life*, Tsaile: Navajo Community College Press, 1977, p. 25.
11. Kaufman, Henry, "Financial Derivatives and their Risks", a talk delivered before City of London Conference on Derivatives, London, England, October 14, 1993.

APPENDIX A

Reserve Requirements of Depository Institutions

Type of deposit[2]	Requirements	
	Percent of deposits	Effective date
Net transaction accounts[3]		
$0 million–$46.8 million	3	12/15/92
More than $46.8 million	10	12/15/92
Nonpersonal time deposits[4]	0	12/27/90
Eurocurrency liabilities[5]	0	12/27/90

1. Reserve requirements in effect on December 31, 1992. Required reserves must be held in the form of deposits with Federal Reserve Banks or vault cash. Nonmember institutions may maintain reserve balances with a Federal Reserve Bank indirectly on a pass-through basis with certain approved institutions. For previous reserve requirements, see earlier editions of the *Annual Report* or the *Federal Reserve Bulletin.* Under provisions of the Monetary Control Act, depository institutions include commercial banks, mutual savings banks, savings and loan associations, credit unions, agencies and branches of foreign banks, and Edge corporations.

2. The Garn–St Germain Depository Institutions Act of 1982 (Public Law 97–320) requires that $2 million of reservable liabilities of each depository institution be subject to a zero percent reserve requirement. The Board is to adjust the amount of reservable liabilities subject to this zero percent reserve requirement each year for the succeeding calendar year by 80 percent of the percentage increase in the total reservable liabilities of all depository institutions measured on an annual basis as of June 30. No corresponding adjustment is to be made in the event of a decrease. On December 15, 1992, the exemption was raised from $3.6 million to $3.8 million. The exemption applies in the following order: (1) net negotiable order of withdrawal (NOW) accounts (NOW accounts less allowable deductions); and (2) net other transaction accounts. The exemption applies only to accounts that would be subject to a 3 percent reserve requirement.

3. Transaction accounts include all deposits against which the account holder is permitted to make withdrawals by negotiable or transferable instruments, payment orders of withdrawal, and telephone and preauthorized transfers in excess of three per month for the purpose of making payments to third persons or others. However, money market deposit accounts (MMDAs) and similar accounts subject to the rules that permit no more than six preauthorized, automatic, or other transfers per month, of which no more than three can be checks, are not transaction accounts (such accounts are savings deposits).

The Monetary Control Act of 1980 requires that the amount of transaction accounts against which the 3 percent reserve requirement applies be modified annually by 80 percent of the percentage change in transaction accounts held by all depository institutions, determined as of June 30 each year. Effective December 15, 1992 for institutions reporting quarterly and December 22, 1992 for institutions reporting weekly, the amount was increased from $42.2 million to $46.8 million.

4. For institutions that report weekly, the reserve requirement on nonpersonal time deposits with an original maturity of less than 1½ years was reduced from 3 percent to 1½ percent for the maintenance period that began December 13, 1990, and to zero for the maintenance period that began December 27, 1990. The reserve requirement on nonpersonal time deposits with an original maturity of 1½ years or more has been zero since October 6, 1983.

For institutions that report quarterly, the reserve requirement on nonpersonal time deposits with an original maturity of less than 1½ years was reduced from 3 percent to zero on January 17, 1991.

5. The reserve requirement on Euroccurency liabilities was reduced from 3 percent to zero in the same manner and on the same dates as were the reserve requirement on nonpersonal time deposits with an original maturity of less than 1½ years (see note 4).

BIBLIOGRAPHY

Angell, Norman, *The Story of Money*. New York: Frederick A. Stokes Co., 1929.

Beck, Peggy V. and Walters, Anne L., *The Sacred: Ways of Knowledge Sources of Life*. Tsaile: Navajo Community College Press, 1977.

Biddell, Jack L., *A Self-Reliant Future for Canada*. Thornhill: LNC Publications, 1993.

Campbell, Alexander, *The True Greenback*. Chicago: Republican Books, 1868.

Capie, Forrest H. (ed.), *Major Inflations in History*. Aldershot: Edward Elgar Publishing Ltd., 1991, pp. 210-212.

Caves, Richard E., *American Industry: Structure, Conduct, Performance*, 7th ed. Englewood Cliffs: Prentice-Hall Inc., 1992.

Chaffers, William, *Gilda Aurifabrorum: A History of English Goldsmiths and Plateworkers, and Their Marks Stamped on Plate*. London: Reeves & Turner, [1800].

Cowles, Virginia, *The Rothschilds: A Family of Fortune*. New York: Alfred A. Knopf, Inc, 1973.

Day, Donald, *Will Rogers: A Biography*. New York: David McKay Company, Inc., 1962.

Deane, Marjorie, and Pringle, Robert, *The Central Banks*. London: Hamish Hamilton Ltd., 1994.

Ferguson, E. James, *The Power of the Purse: A History of American Public Finance, 1776-1790*. Chapel Hill: University of North Carolina Press, 1961.

Fisher, Irving, *100% Money*. New York: The Adelphi Company, 1935.

Franklin, Benjamin, *The Writings of Benjamin Franklin*, Smyth, Albert Henry (ed.). New York: Macmillan, 1907.

Friedman, Milton, *Monetarist Economics*. Oxford: Basil Blackwell Ltd., 1991.

Friedman, Milton, *A Program for Monetary Stability*. New York: Fordham University Press, 1959.

Friedman, Milton, and Friedman, Rose D., *Free to Choose: A Personal Statement*. New York: Harcourt Brace Jovanovich, Inc., 1981.

Friedman, Milton and Schwartz, Anna Jacobson, *A Monetary History of the United States 1867-1960*. Princeton: Princeton University Press, 1963.

Galbraith, John Kenneth, *A Journey Through Economic Time: A Firsthand View*. New York: Houghton Mifflin Company, 1994.

Galbraith, John Kenneth, *Money, Whence it Came, Where it Went*. Boston: Houghton Mifflin Company, 1975.

Galbraith, John Kenneth, *The New Industrial State*. Boston: Houghton Mifflin Co., 1971.

Gouge, William M., *A Short History of Paper Money and Banking in the United States*. New York: Augustus M. Kelley, 1968.

Hammond, Bray, *Sovereignty and an Empty Purse*. Princeton: Princeton University Press, 1970.

Hellyer, Paul, *Exit Inflation*. Toronto: Nelson Canada Limited, 1981.

Henderson, David R. (ed.), *The Fortune Encyclopedia of Economics*. New York: Warner Books, Inc., 1993.

Hixson, William F., *Triumph of the Bankers: Money and Banking in the Eighteenth and Nineteenth Centuries*. Westport: Praeger Publishers, 1993.

Innis, Mary Quayle, *An Economic History of Canada*. Toronto: The Ryerson Press, 1935.

Jones, Aubrey, *The New Inflation: The Politics of Prices and Incomes*. London: Andre Deutsch, 1973.

Lekachman, Robert, *Inflation: The Permanent Problem of Boom and Bust*. New York: Vintage Books, 1973.

Low, Richard E. (ed.), *The Economics of Antitrust: Competition and Monopoly*. Englewood Cliffs: Prentice-Hall Inc., 1968.

Lui, Francis T., *Major Inflations in History*, Capie, Forrest H. (ed.). Aldershot: Edward Elgar Publishing Ltd., 1991.

Lux, Kenneth, *Adam Smith's Mistake: How a Moral Philosopher Invented Economics and Ended Morality*. Boston: Shambhala Publications Inc., 1990.

McCarthy, W.E.J., O'Brien, J.F., and V.G. Dowd, *Wage Inflation and Wage Leadership: A Study of the Role of Key Wage Bargains in the Irish System of Collective Bargaining*. Dublin: Cahill & Co. Ltd., 1975.

McCulloch, Hugh, *Men and Measures of Half a Century*. New York: Charles Scribner's Sons, 1888.

McIvor, R. Craig, *Canadian Monetary, Banking and Fiscal Development*. Toronto: The Macmillan Company of Canada Limited, 1958.

McPherson, Edward (ed.), *A Handbook of Politics*. New York: Da Capo Publishing Corp., 1972.

Metcalf, Jack, *The Two Hundred Year Debate: Who Shall Issue the Nation's Money*. Olympia: An Honest Money for America Publication, 1986.

Mill, John Stuart, *Principles of Political Economy with some of their Applications to Social Philosophy*. New York: Augustus M. Kelley, 1909.

Millman, Gregory J., *The Valdals' Crown: How Rebel Currency Traders Overthrew the World's Central Banks*. New York: The Free Press, 1995.

Morris, Richard B., *The Forging of the Union 1781-1789*. New York: Harper & Row, 1987.

Munkirs, John R., *The Transformation of American Capitalism From Competitive Market Structures to Centralized Private Sector Planning*. New York: M.E. Sharpe, Inc., 1985.

Myers, Margaret G., *A Financial History of the United States*. New York: Columbia University Press, 1970.

Nettles, Curtis P., *The Money Supply of the American Colonies before 1720*. New York: Augustus M. Kelley, 1964.

Nicolay, John G., and Hay, John (eds.), *Abraham Lincoln: Complete Works*. New York: The Century Co., 1907.

Powell, Ellis T., *The Evolution of the Money Market – 1385-1915*. New York: Augustus M. Kelley, 1966.

Samuelson, Paul A., *Economics*, 9th ed. New York: McGraw-Hill Book Co., 1973.

Saul, John Ralston, *Voltaire's Bastards: The Dictatorship of Reason in the West*. Toronto: Penguin Books, 1992.

Schumacher, Ernst F., *Small is Beautiful: Economics as if People Mattered*. New York: Harper & Row, Publishers, Inc., 1989.

Simons, Henry C., *Economic Policy for a Free Society*. Chicago: University of Chicago Press, 1948.

Solomon, Steven, *The Confidence Game: How Unelected Central Bankers Are Governing the Changed Global Economy*. New York: Simon & Schuster, 1995.

Smith, Adam, *The Wealth of Nations*, Cannan, Edwin (ed.). New York: Modern Library, 1937.

Steinbach, Alexander Alan, *What is Judaism*. New York: Behrman Jewish Book House, 1937

Sumner, William Graham, *A History of American Currency*. New York: Augustus M. Kelley, 1968.

Weintraub, Sidney, *Capitalism's Inflation and Unemployment Crisis: Beyond Monetarism and Keynesiasm*. New York: Addison-Wesley Publishing Co. Inc., 1978.

INDEX